the
new teacher's
companion

SUSTAINABLE
FORESTRY
INITIATIVE

Certified Fiber Sourcing

www.sfiprogram.org

the new teacher's companion

PRACTICAL WISDOM FOR SUCCEEDING IN THE CLASSROOM

Gini Cunningham

...

ASCD

Alexandria, Virginia USA

1703 N. Beauregard St. • Alexandria, VA 22311-1714 USA
Phone: 800-933-2723 or 703-578-9600 • Fax: 703-575-5400
Web site: www.ascd.org • E-mail: member@ascd.org
Author guidelines: www.ascd.org/write

Gene R. Carter, *Executive Director;* Nancy Modrak, *Publisher;* Scott Willis, *Director, Book Acquisitions & Development;* Carolyn Pool, *Acquisitions Editor;* Julie Houtz, *Director, Book Editing & Production;* Darcie Russell, *Editor;* Catherine Guyer, *Senior Graphic Designer;* Mike Kalyan, *Production Manager;* Marlene Hochberg, *Typesetter;* Carmen Yuhas, *Production Specialist*

Printed in the United States of America. Cover art © 2009 by ASCD. ASCD publications present a variety of viewpoints. The views expressed or implied in this book should not be interpreted as official positions of the Association.

All Web links in this book are correct as of the publication date below but may have become inactive or otherwise modified since that time. If you notice a deactivated or changed link, please e-mail books@ascd.org with the words "Link Update" in the subject line. In your message, please specify the Web link, the book title, and the page number on which the link appears.

PAPERBACK ISBN: 978-1-4166-0882-0   ASCD product #109051   n11/09

Also available as an e-book (see Books in Print for the ISBNs)

Quantity discounts for the paperback edition only: 10–49 copies, 10%; 50+ copies, 15%; for 1,000 or more copies, call 800-933-2723, ext. 5634, or 703-575-5634. For desk copies: member@ascd.org.

Library of Congress Cataloging-in-Publication Data

Cunningham, Gini.
  The new teacher's companion : practical wisdom for succeeding in the classroom / Gini Cunningham.
      p. cm.
  Includes bibliographical references and index.
  ISBN 978-1-4166-0882-0 (pbk. : alk. paper) 1. First year teachers–United States. 2. Teacher effectiveness–United States. 3. Effective teaching–United States. I. Title.

  LB2844.1.N4C86 2009
  371.102–dc22

                          2009026224

20 19 18 17 16 15 14 13 12 11 10 09   1 2 3 4 5 6 7 8 9 10 11 12

To Lynn—an educator, coach, and
role model of excellence

To TW, Stan, and Allison—my children
who enrich my life daily

the new teacher's companion

PRACTICAL WISDOM FOR SUCCEEDING IN THE CLASSROOM

Foreword

• • •

When I was offered my first teaching job in the late 1970s, I was excited to be embarking on the career I had planned for since I was a little girl. As the beginning of the new school year approached, my anticipation and excitement were joined by a heavy sense of the responsibility and lists of requirements of my new teaching job. Although I had gone to an innovative college where I was "prepared" to be a teacher through a four-year practicum-based program with incredible professors and vast amounts of hands-on experience ... I wasn't ready. No one is. My emotions are still vivid.

I had no idea that as a new teacher, I would cry every day (including weekends) for at least two months. Although I (usually) didn't cry at school, by the time I got to my car—and definitely by the time I got home—I could count on feeling desperate, despondent, and deficient.

Don't misunderstand. I loved being a teacher. I couldn't possibly have put in more time at school and at home to be "ready." I brought my best self to school each day. Yet I felt so alone in what I was doing. Sadly, I had no way of knowing that what I was experiencing was normal. Needless to say, there was no mentoring program set up for our school district.

I wish I had been able to access a compassionate, clever, and considerate mentor and guide who could provide the tips, tales, tools, and techniques that a novice teacher needs to feel at least a modicum of success day-to-day. All teachers who are beginning in the profession, as well as those switching to a different type of school or school district, need a special someone who can help with

- setting up, maintaining, and managing the classroom;
- getting along with other teachers;
- working with parents;
- planning for an ever-changing and increasingly rigorous curriculum;
- handling the stresses of being under the scrutiny of administrators, parents, other teachers, and of course, the students;
- managing and optimizing time and talents;
- remembering the real reason we chose to become teachers; and
- dealing with the myriad other demands of being an educator in the 21st century.

What new teachers really need is someone who is right there with us, before school, during the school day, after school, and on the weekends. We need to know we can ask questions of this sage advisor, trusting that our questions will be neither seen as silly nor shared with others in the teachers' lounge (or anywhere else). The truth of the matter is, of course, that no school district can provide a 24/7/365 resource person for each new teacher.

All is not lost because now we have this book from master teacher and guide Gini Cunningham. She is the mentor that new teachers need. Every new teacher can benefit from her wisdom any time of the day or night, not just the educators who are fortunate enough to work one-on-one with her.

Gini's book is magical for new teachers for so many reasons. A few of the reasons that you'll discover:

- She tells stories that are real, comforting, and pull you right into the experience.
- Her passion for teaching is communicated tenderly yet eloquently so that every reader is convinced that teaching is the finest profession and is a career selection made with both the heart and mind.
- The practicality of Gini's suggestions is encouraging. Too many books share the tribulations, which seem impossible to surmount to a new teacher, whereas Gini shares realistic tips and successes.
- Whether you need advice on one topic in the middle of the night or an overview of advice in the middle of the afternoon, the book is accessible when you need it. Jump into the pages to find Gini's suggestions and support on numerous critical topics.

I've heard it said that we should have one mentor who is twice our age and one mentor who is half our age. Somehow, with Gini Cunningham, you get both. She has the wisdom that comes only through living and experiencing what life has to offer. She also brings a youth and freshness to her conversations and relationships. These qualities come through in her writing; I don't know anyone else like her.

Every teacher has experienced the pain and trials of the anticipated and dreaded first year of teaching. Given that shared experience, we all know that Gini's advice is needed and more than a welcome addition to the literature and materials weighing down the briefcases, bookshelves, and desks of new teachers. Keep learning with each reading of this book; share it with others who are, work with, or are getting ready to join the ranks of new teachers. Read, learn, and enjoy!

Meggin McIntosh
Professor Emerita, University of Nevada, Reno
www.meggin.com

Acknowledgments

• • •

This book became a reality through the power and support of many people. Dr. Meggin McIntosh believed in me and my writing from the first day I set my fingers on the keyboard. Her laughs and insight have ignited me. My editors at ASCD—Scott Willis, Carolyn Pool, and Darcie Russell—have offered their vast knowledge of writing and publishing. Their input has strengthened my joy with words as revealed through the teaching tips and experiences offered here. Thanks to my parents, William and Eleanor Lipscomb. Earliest memories of them include playing educational games in the car or around the dinner table. This love of learning has guided me throughout my schooling and teaching and is the essential foundation of an education. My sisters offered amazing support during my writing: Marilyn constantly reminded me to remember my audience and their needs; Judy shed her experiences of teaching and tied them to mine; Jackie always cheered the worth of my work.

More than 50 years of learning are stamped into these pages. Excellent teachers and enlightening coworkers plus thousands of delightful and challenging students have channeled my learning and love of teaching. Thanks to my first mentors who set me on the road to teaching success, Gail McNeill and Shelley Tronstad; to Arlene Myers, who inspired me with the significance of writing and words; to Rosita Kottke, who exemplifies teaching every student to reach the greatest learning expectations; to Gail Janhunen, who shows me magic in the classroom every day; and to Karen Ash, who has acted as a sounding board and partner as we shared hundreds of adventures with new teachers. I hope that every teacher will be wrapped in the thrill and excitement of educating students, building knowledge, and expanding skills that carry over into lifelong success. No profession can match the wonder of working with young minds.

My children, TW, Stan, and Allison, are tapped into every word. I appreciate the wonder and joy they have brought me, the lessons they have shared with me, and their unique ways of learning and applying knowledge. My husband, Lynn, has provided unwavering faith in me.

Introduction

• • •

Courses in college, supervised teaching, and animated discussions with friends only begin to prepare you for actually being a full-time, certified teacher. Every day on the job you will grow and learn from experiences that come from being an instructional leader. Something magical happens when you work with dedicated colleagues and eager students. As the excitement and thrill of teaching escalate, confidence and competence expand. Educating students is filled with challenges and successes that turn a "regular" job into total fulfillment.

Over the years, I've experienced many of these challenges. One of the most memorable occurred when I was teaching physical education at an elementary school. With a sick and weeping student at my side, midway through my effort to mop up a pool of vomit on the floor, I dodged as a chair came hurtling toward my legs. As I shook disinfectant powder on the gooey remains and patted Trina gently on the back, I glared at Willie-the-Chair-Boy. I then calmly asked Paul to dash to the office to get me some help. As things were just about to return to normal, Freddy tripped over Anna, embedding his two new front teeth into her skull.

Anna stumbled toward me with tears in her eyes, and a quick examination of her head revealed why she was crying. Blood was seeping from the head bite, while across the room Freddy was yanking long strands of hair from in between his teeth.

At this exact moment the gym door exploded open and thunder rattled the building. In came a soaking-wet Cindy, the neighborhood dog who adored kids, loved to wander, and detested loud noises. The dog's sudden entrance diverted the attention of all 37 of my 2nd graders, but eventually I gathered the class together to proceed as normally as possible with scooter board hockey, our game of the day.

Such is the start of a day in the life of an elementary physical education teacher, and all of this before 9:00 a.m.! Who could imagine what else might be in store on this day? At lunch, the classroom teachers of my 2nd grade students arrived at my door, with wide-eyed children clutching their hands. "They were worried about you," Mrs. Stevens announced. "It sounds like you had quite a morning!" As if on cue, the youngsters let go of their teachers, ran toward me, and enveloped me with hugs of love.

Is there a more demanding and yet fulfilling profession on earth than teaching? Every day in the classroom brings love and learning. Students and teachers who care about one another and about you are a powerful part of a thrilling career.

The Purpose of This Book

Administrators hire the best teachers they can find for the positions they have available. Some teachers arrive with excellent training and years of experience that make the transition into the new job quite simple. Others enter the classroom as "boss" for the first time. They may be confused, scared, and ill-prepared for the real world of teaching. This book is intended to assist new teachers during the first days, weeks, and months of that crucial first year of teaching, to ensure that they are ready for the challenges of the job, equipped with the background knowledge and support that will maintain their enthusiasm while they develop the talents that will keep them in the profession for many years to come.

The tips and tales in this book come from my own experience, direct observation, or lessons taught and shared by teachers. Based on years of interaction with hundreds of colleagues and thousands of students, every idea has helped to improve classroom instruction and student learning. Although there is never one perfect answer for every situation, there are definitely guidelines that can help teachers and students succeed while avoiding potential pitfalls. Great teaching from the start of the school year to the end is the result of thorough planning, preparation, and dedication to being the best teacher possible. This book entertains, guides, and supports new teachers as they work to get everything just right.

In many ways, the new teacher launching a career is like a person standing in front of the map in the mall, looking at the big "You Are Here" label. You know where you are, you are fairly sure of how you got there, and now you have hundreds (maybe thousands) of choices and decisions to make as the first year of teaching unfolds and you realize the enormity of the job. New teachers have completed college and all of the requirements, and often teaching has been made to look quite simple. The teacher teaches, the students learn, day one leads to day one hundred, and so on throughout the year. During student teaching, students behaved, colleagues and parents respected teacher expertise, and confidence abounded. Now, on the job, the reality and responsibility of the assignment really hit home.

The Real World of Teaching

The real world of teaching may appear somewhat different than the dream world, especially in the beginning. The new teacher is now in charge of every facet of instruction, plus many other aspects of the job. That is why summer planning and advance preparation are absolutely essential. Administrators are often overwhelmed with the many other demands of running the school, and although they would like to spend hours in every classroom, that is an impossibility. The guidelines in *The New Teacher's Companion* give new teachers much-needed assistance as they launch their career.

Although teachers may have a kind and caring spouse or significant other, completely supportive children, and newfound, helpful teaching colleagues, when the bell rings and they enter the classroom, they are, in many ways, completely alone. That independence is one of the benefits of teaching, but it can also be extremely frightening. Teaching entails vast responsibility for instruction that supports the growth and development of every learner. Research confirms that the teacher makes the greatest difference in the learning success of students. Can any school or administrator risk not having excellence in every classroom from the outset? Would any teacher wish to be less than fully equipped and qualified for the job?

The most positive starts come from independent preparation, planning, and research on instruction and learning, coupled with discussion and sharing with administrators and colleagues. By reading this book, jotting down notes, determining goals for achievement in learning, and dreaming about making a difference in the lives of children, new teachers set themselves up for success. The teaching profession, overflowing with stress and intense responsibility, packed with hundreds of daily challenges, is neither simple nor easy. But it is richly satisfying. Theory is great for expanding thinking, but practical tips and real-world anecdotes such as those offered in this book are invaluable.

Format and Features

The book is written especially for new teachers who are excitedly preparing for their first job—and also for the administrators who just did the hiring—and the mentors and coworkers who want to make the new teacher's transition smooth. All student names and some adult names are pseudonyms. All individuals mentioned have greatly influenced my life and my teaching.

Each chapter begins with a brief summary of main ideas and a review of the main points of the preceding chapter, followed by sections titled The Challenge and Lessons Learned, which introduce the new chapter material with real stories as anecdotes. The story at the beginning of this chapter about my 2nd grade physical education class is an example of a challenge and a lesson learned. Sections I think of as true tales, marked with stylized puzzle pieces, are linked to the key points of a chapter and are woven into the text. Teaching is a deeply personal and moving profession, generating an abundance of amazing adventures and remarkable experiences. These stories serve as background information for teachers as they begin to accumulate their own teaching experiences.

The body of the chapter consists of tips and ideas to aid new teachers during the critical first year of the job. In addition to new teachers, administrators will find these tips and ideas to be a handy guide to support new professionals as they strive for teaching excellence—an important task, given the huge turnover of new teachers within the first five years of teaching. Although it is essential to modify and adjust the tips to match individual needs and particular teaching assignments, the essence of each focuses on excellence of instruction and the achievement of all students. Each chapter also has messages marked with a heart that are intended as additional gentle nudges toward excellence. Closing Advice at the end of each chapter summarizes key points and adds final insight. Lists throughout the book provide a handy way to check and double-check understanding and to guide planning and preparation.

At the end of the book is a list of References and Resources to further support learning and extend the knowledge of new teachers. The appendixes provide additional material for planning and preparation.

About the Chapters

Chapters 1 through 4 are intended to assist with initial preparation for teaching, including many tasks to be done before the first student arrives. The topics covered include the following:

- Developing a personal vision, beliefs, and goals for teaching
- Learning about and understanding school and district policies
- Establishing classroom rules that maintain discipline
- Deciding consequences for misbehavior and how they will be administered

Chapters 5 and 6 offer suggestions for organizing the classroom and planning for various procedures. Topics covered include the following:

- Determining appropriate rewards and awards to honor and promote learning
- Designing the layout and organization of the classroom
- Planning for every anticipated classroom procedure
- Organizing textbooks, trade books, instructional materials, and supplies for creating excellent lessons
- Creating seating charts, name tags, and other identifiers to start the year with ease

Chapters 7 through 9 cover topics that focus on the essentials of excellent instruction, including the following:

- Creating lesson plans that are clear, coordinated, and planned for student success
- Integrating daily lessons into unit plans that coordinate and sequence learning
- Understanding time management so that every minute in the classroom is well paced and filled with learning
- Knowing and using student engagement strategies to verify each student's learning and degree of understanding of every lesson component

Chapters 10 and 11 provide additional information for teachers to ensure that students have learned by reiterating the essential question: What do my students really know, and what are they able to do? The teacher uses the answers to this question to determine the following: What do I do now to advance the learning of students who "get it," and how shall I review and reteach for students who do not "get it yet"? Determining the answers to these questions involves the following activities:

• Assessing student learning and understanding, pinpointing misconceptions, and adjusting future lessons to meet student needs

• Creating minilessons to meet student learning needs

• Writing and asking deep-thinking questions to promote understanding

• Generating ways for students to respond to extend knowledge and create independent learners and thinkers

• Grading student work fairly and efficiently with adequate feedback to increase understanding

• Developing students who are able to self-assess and determine the next steps in learning as they move toward becoming independent learners

The book concludes with Chapter 12, a roundup of key ideas and final reminders for teaching excellence.

• • • • • • • •

Teaching is a wonderful adventure. Great administrators want their teachers and students to achieve excellence. Students learn from great teachers, and great teachers continue to learn every day from their students, from research, from colleagues, from experience, and from the drive to reach and teach all the children with whom they work. Keeping in mind that no class, no subject, no student or group of students, and no day is ever the same, the key ideas in *The New Teacher's Companion* make high-quality instruction possible from the outset. Great teachers really do make a difference. No other profession can compete with the magic of teaching!

1

Teaching—
It's More Than a Job, It's Magic

• • •

Ideally, administrators have a vision for each new teacher they hire, characterized by teaching excellence and high levels of student achievement. In turn, new teachers need a clear vision for their teaching plans and the learning success of all students. Acknowledging beliefs about students and learning and establishing goals for student achievement help to refine instructional effort and turn the vision into reality.

By examining personal beliefs and goals and creating a vision, teachers clarify where they are headed so that they can efficiently design how to get there. This self-analysis and additional discussion with colleagues and administrators solidify the vision while creating positive school relationships.

The Challenge

I was loading cases of pop for the vending machine onto a cart in the tiny storage room when the disaster occurred. As I pulled one of the cartons down from the high stack, it ripped open, and soon one falling can led to another until soda was spewing everywhere around the room, dripping off the ceiling, dribbling down the walls, and puddling across the floor. There I stood, Dr Pepper trickling down my legs and off my nose and hair and a splattered display across my dress. If I had planned it, I could not have created a bigger, stickier mess! And the worst part was that all of this came on the heels of one of the most disappointing days of my teaching career.

A student had been withdrawn from my class. It sounds simple, but it was so terrible to have him removed from my roll. He was a very bright boy, but we had butted heads several times over assignments and classroom rules. The final blow came when he walked between idling school buses instead of going around them on our return from the public library. In this case, his disregard of the rules was simply dangerous.

To make the situation even more heart-wrenching for me, he was the son of teacher-colleagues. I really wanted to make things right with him. To have him leave my classroom reflected failure in my teaching, even though his parents had told me, "It is for the best." This stubborn streak, an inability to admit defeat, is something that runs deep in me. Sticking to it (literally and figuratively) is how I operate, even though this attitude is not always for the best.

As my anguished tears began to tumble and mix with my view of the mess in the storage room, I reevaluated my position and wondered about any other possible job that would not break my heart. At that precise instant coworker Todd Holden waltzed into the messy pool with a booming "Howdy!" His warm smile disintegrated into dismay as he surveyed the catastrophe. "How can I help?" he kindly asked. Those words of support changed my day and reversed my attitude almost immediately.

Lessons Learned

Teaching does not always run perfectly, but with reflection and the support of friendly colleagues, it all can be made right. Every day is a day of learning for students and teachers alike. On that day I learned to handle disappointments by facing them and then moving forward doing something I love—teaching. Realizing I could not please everyone all the time, I did know that I could make a difference for students who needed the knowledge and skills of reading, writing, and thinking I offered. That is what this profession is all about—teaching children, learning with them and from them, and accepting the responsibility of making a difference for their futures.

Planning for Excellence in Teaching

Being a teacher is far more than a job, a duty, or a paycheck. It is a calling. This calling provides the opportunity to work with learners as they advance through school. Teachers watch students grow and develop intellectually, guiding them as they tackle new concepts and ideas and leading them as they become self-sufficient and independent learners. The lessons that are taught, the methods that are incorporated, and the attitudes of teachers toward their students and toward learning have a lasting influence on life.

Teaching is definitely hard work. From preschoolers to seniors in high school, despite the difference in age, all students are just children full of potential and curiosity, waiting for their teacher to empower their learning and extend their knowledge. Good instruction from teachers who care promotes success in learning.

Vision for Teaching and Learning

Good teachers come to school and teach students who learn a little. Great teachers have clear goals and a big vision for students to learn and achieve at high levels. Creating a mind map of this vision of teaching provides a foundational guide for the year. Notes and descriptions can be added and adjustments made as needed. Figure 1.1 shows components essential for successful teaching. By studying and reflecting on each one, you will be better prepared for teaching. Knowing what you want students

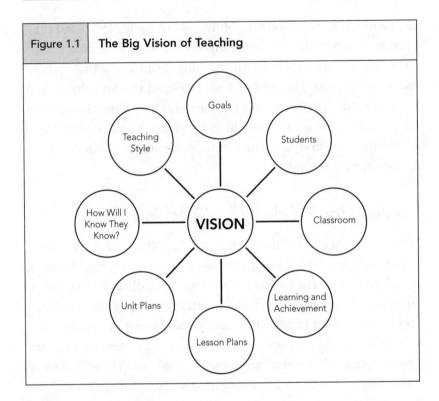

Figure 1.1 — The Big Vision of Teaching

to know and to be able to do, and how you plan to get it done, guides you in a direction to arrive at the final destination—successful student learning.

As you reflect on various components of the vision, consider questions such as these:

- Why is this important?
- How will I get this accomplished?
- What problems might I encounter and when?
- What indicators will tell me I have succeeded?

This vision acts as a reminder of the broad scope of responsibilities to be addressed during the school year.

Reflecting on the elements of the vision provides the self-knowledge necessary to fill in a sample chart, such as the one presented in Figure 1.2. In addition to your vision, use the basic grid to capture your beliefs, goals, and hoped-for achievements. Of course, experiences and unforeseen surprises will suggest

Figure 1.2	Sample Vision, Belief, Goals, and Achievement

Vision of Myself and My Teaching
- The classroom is organized.
- I understand the standards.
- I'm ready to teach.
- I have a sense of sanity because I have succeeded.
- I'm immensely smarter because of this experience.

Beliefs About Myself
- I can meet any challenge.
- I know and understand students, learning, and teaching.
- I know where to get help and when to ask for it.
- I will be a better person as a result of teaching students.

Goals for Myself
- Teach and reach all students.
- Grow and develop teaching skills every day.
- Feel successful in what I have taught.
- Learn every day—from students, peers, reading, research, writing.

How Will I Achieve It All?
- Have clear lesson and unit plans.
- Adjust lessons to meet the needs of my students.
- Assess during lessons so no student is lost.
- Learn everything I can about being a great teacher.

Vision of My Students as They Learn
- Students are eager, excited, exhilarated by learning.
- Learning goals are accomplished at all levels.
- Students are independent learners and willing to challenge themselves.

Beliefs About My Students and Learning
- All students are capable of learning.
- Students want to learn.
- All students want to succeed.
- Students need me.

Goals for My Students
- All students will grow as learners.
- Students will expand their love of learning.
- Students will expand their academic knowledge.
- Students will gain skills and understand concepts that will bring them lifelong success.

How Will I Help Every Student Achieve?
- Teach great lessons.
- Provide well-planned assessments.
- Constantly analyze lessons and learning.
- Carefully use the pacing calendar and curriculum so that learning goals can be met.

changes as your first year of teaching progresses. The first year (and every ensuing year) will be bursting with learning. A truly great teacher learns and grows every day.

Although the detailed responses of different individuals will vary, the ultimate goal is always the successful learning of students through excellent instructional strategies and guidance by the teacher. Planning as well as reflection on vision and goals add certainty to success.

"These darn kids. They just do not want to learn!"

"By golly, I taught it, and still 20 out of 23 failed the test!"

"I'm counting the days until spring break. This is the worst bunch of students I have ever had!"

If vacation is the only thing on a teacher's mind and the thought is not just the result of the exhaustive effort poured into every teaching moment, perhaps it is time to seek another job. If you hear negative words muttered by disgruntled colleagues, the best thing to do is to run! You must teach the students you have with the abilities and background that they possess when they arrive in your classroom. When you believe that every one wants to learn and succeed, you will find that students reflect your optimism.

Every day in teaching, whether it is the most glorious or the toughest, is critical to the success of students. When you expect the best behavior, intellectual output, and scholarly interaction, your goals are more likely to be achieved. Faith in students' capabilities and their desire to grow empowers students as it strengthens your talents and expertise.

Amber was a lovely little 1st grader, full of smiles but low in confidence. In kindergarten she had been labeled as a slow learner. Although the teacher had tried to disguise labeling, Amber sensed it, lived it, and suffered.

Amber's new teacher demanded excellence while designing avenues of individualized learning to help students succeed. Each day Amber gained more confidence. In mid-September, she pulled her teacher aside and whispered, "Mrs. Janhunen, when I got here I wasn't very smart. But you are making me smart. Thanks." Then Amber gently kissed her teacher's hand.

Responsibility and Teaching

As you think about the various factors that affect the elements in the grid in Figure 1.2, a critical question to ask yourself is this: Are you responsible enough to be a teacher who makes a difference in the lives and learning of children?

The goal is not to be an all-right teacher or a good teacher, but the absolute best. To determine this, take the following true-or-false test. (Oh, yes. As a teacher you must love to take tests as well as give them!) The thinking behind each answer reveals much about you, your vision, and your beliefs about teaching.

Teachers are 100 percent responsible for

- Being organized and prepared for every lesson, every day.
- Preparing instruction that ensures learning for all.
- Designing lessons that educate students.
- Checking for understanding throughout the lesson.
- Finding and implementing a variety of activities, strategies, and teaching methods.
- Accepting that all students do not learn the same way or at the same rate.
- Reteaching as needed to help all students learn.
- Enriching each lesson to captivate and motivate learners.
- Caring deeply for every student.
- Realizing that some things just do not work, even with the best of planning.
- Picking up the pieces, loose ends, confusion, and misconceptions of learning and then uncovering ways to correct them.
- Starting each day fresh, excited, and dedicated to students.
- Ending each day by looking forward to tomorrow with enthusiasm and dedication.
- Knowing that what they say, do, teach, and model affects every student now and forever.
- Believing that *no other job* is as important as being a teacher.

Knowing that you have responded to each statement with a "true," I've saved the toughest question for last. True or false? Teachers are 100 percent responsible for

- Making all students learn.

Finally, a false! This one is impossible. No teacher can force students to do anything. However, students are relying on the expert knowledge and dedicated instruction of their teacher to help them learn. No child wants to be a failure or to appear incapable. Your students depend on you.

I spent many years "forcing" students to learn. Even though in my heart I knew that they had to want to learn, to see the value of learning, I still pushed them hard—almost relentlessly. With experience I figured out that I needed to provide students with more ways to own their learning, through opportunities like self-selected reading and writing for reflection on learning. With prodding and encouragement, my students grew in independence and competence, knowing that I not only acted as a guide for learning but also honored and respected their insight and feedback. When you ask your students about what they know, you receive so much information in return.

Owning learning is evidenced when students are allowed to solve problems, explain events, and create products that demonstrate their understanding. Allowing students to own their learning means that you must be ready to accept multiple ways of discovering answers—answers that are not necessarily the same but that are plausible, or responses that with adjustments to correct misconceptions lead to learning that develops independence. In math class, owning learning might be demonstrated through multiple ways of solving a problem; in poetry it might be evident in different interpretations of the author's meaning; in woodshop it might be students constructing similar projects but selecting a variety of materials, designs, and finishing techniques. If you, the teacher, always provide one right answer, why would students ever need to really think?

Closing Advice

Teachers have the powerful responsibility of influencing student lives and learning. While this is ominous, to say the least, it is richly rewarding as you transport students to higher understanding and achievement. With a vision of excellence coupled with hard work, extreme effort, and the solid belief that all students are capable, you will discover many miracle-filled moments generated by the excitement of your teaching and your students' desire to learn.

Each day you will also realize many things about yourself as you discover talents that perhaps even you did not know you have. As you challenge student minds to stretch and grow, you will find that you are exploding with new ideas to help students succeed. Though exhausting on the best of days, your teaching and caring about your students offer vitality and thrills that continuously replenish your energy.

2

You've Got the Job! Now Deal with the Business Details

• • •

You have been hired, the ink on the contract is dry, and you come to your new assignment prepared with a fairly good idea of what teaching is all about. In reality, however, new teachers are unleashed into an adventure of unimaginable proportions. College courses, in-class observations, supervised student teaching, and previous job experience support teachers in many ways, but real teaching in your own classroom with real students is an amazing and challenging undertaking.

Before you can begin teaching, you need to attend to the business side of a teaching contract by getting answers to questions, submitting all paperwork, and making sure you understand important school and district policies. Taking the time to cover outside-of-the-classroom responsibilities before school starts leaves you ample time to focus on your teaching when the bell sounds, and it rids you of potential stress because you know all the details and expectations of your job. Although policies vary by school and district, new teachers need to know about and take care of critical items in several general categories.

School and District Rules and Regulations

Each school and district has manuals, books, and other guides to help teachers transition into the job. Copies may be handed to teachers by the hiring committee, or they may be available in the classroom, from the office manager, or from other authorized personnel. Policy manuals contain absolutely vital information about the operation and expectations of each school and district. Read them carefully.

One of your priorities as a new teacher should be checking to make sure your teaching certificate and credentialed qualifications match the position for which you have been hired. This also includes checking on required district and state courses, examinations, forms to be completed, and more.

Teacher Certification and Recertification Requirements

Answer the following questions to ensure that your job qualifications match the position requirements:

- Is your teaching certificate current? When does it expire?
- Are there any provisions—tests, classes, applications—to be completed?
- Which specific teaching assignments match the certification?
- Do all relevant parties have the certificate and necessary paperwork on file—the district, the state department of education, and you, the teacher?

Certification is just the beginning of the business end of the new job, but it is critical to keeping the job (and getting paid). Certification varies from state to state. Do not assume that your California license matches the requirements of Delaware.

Once your certificate arrives, frame it and hang it proudly in your room. You are a professional, so display your degree, awards, and credentials for students, parents, and colleagues to see. Success to this point in life has come from dedication and commitment to excellence—share your achievements.

Mandatory Teaching Examinations

Make sure you have taken all mandatory district and state teaching examinations and know where to send the results. Use these guiding questions as a checklist:

• Have you taken all courses specific to the school, district, and state to meet all requirements as detailed by law or the state constitution?

• Are there national examinations you must pass, such as the Praxis II?

• To whom must you submit scores, and by what date? Track anything you send by mail.

• Do you have a copy of passing scores available in case any questions arise?

Additional Coursework and Credentials

Additional coursework allows teachers to teach more grade levels and subject areas, plus it moves them up on the salary schedule. However, none of this can happen if the district is unaware of these courses and certifications. It is your responsibility to have all paperwork up-to-date and on file. Passing scores and other certification information are most often listed on the teaching credentials. More information about this is available from the certification branch of the department of education of each state.

Some teachers can be cantankerous, especially when they encounter obstacles. One particularly difficult teacher furiously reprimanded a district employee for not informing him that his license would expire on his birthday. Despite the time and energy the teacher spent blaming others, he did not complete the required coursework and applications and eventually lost his certificate. He could continue teaching for the remainder of the year, but only as a substitute teacher, thus relinquishing his teacher salary, district-paid health insurance, tenure, and retirement benefits. The business side of a teaching contract is important. Take care of it.

Other School and District Policies

In addition to a teaching license and certifications, there are many other business items to know about.

State and local standards for academic achievement. Where can you locate the state, district, and school academic standards for the appropriate grade level and subject area? Teaching is based on an established curriculum that follows district, state, and/or national standards. Teachers must know the content responsibilities of the job as described by the standards.

As a new teacher, you must also know the required degree of proficiency for students and the expectations of local and state examinations that assess students against each of these standards. If you do not teach what students must know and be able to do, success for you and your students becomes elusive, if not impossible. (Chapter 3 has more information about becoming familiar with standards.)

Curriculum guides for instruction by grade level and subject area. What are the school and district requirements in each curriculum area being taught? The curriculum has been designed to meet district and state requirements and to help students attain desired outcomes as outlined in the standards. New teachers must know how the curriculum aligns across grade levels and subjects. Studying the curriculum in conjunction with the standards clarifies what students must know and be able to do in all content areas and levels of study.

Pacing charts for instruction. With so much to be taught, new teachers must know how to reach their teaching goals within the allotted time frame of the day, week, and year. Thus it is important to ask if the school or district has an established calendar for teaching and assessing each standard. If so, you can plan the year using the guide, ensuring that all the required material will be covered. If the school or district has no pacing chart, you will need to outline basic daily lessons for the entire year (see Chapter 3 for helpful suggestions on how to do this). These will be adjusted as needed as the school year unfolds.

Mandatory minutes/hours of instruction required. In many districts and schools, certain subject areas—especially reading and mathematics—have a mandatory number of minutes or hours of instruction each day or each week. Knowing these requirements is important to good planning and to meeting school district mandates. This information should be listed in the curriculum, pacing chart, or the school policy manual. By recording the necessary information in your lesson plan book, it is available for reference throughout the year.

School, district, and state assessment expectations and procedures. Testing takes place in every school, and as a new teacher you must be fully aware of the types of assessment the school takes part in—common assessments; teacher-generated assessments; purchased assessments; district, state, and nationally mandated assessments. More specifically, you must know the answers to the following questions:

• When is each district or state assessment given, and when are results received?

• How are the results used to improve future teaching and learning?

• What are the expectations for assessments and the data generated?

In schools that are data driven, teachers need to be aware of how assessments are linked to student achievement. Data indicate students who are proficient as well as students who are not yet proficient and need additional support. With this information, you can adjust lessons to meet the needs of every learner.

Policies and procedures regarding student absences. It is important to know how many days students may miss during a semester or year and if the school or district requires different actions for excused and unexcused absences. Key questions include these:

• Must students bring a signed note after an absence?

• What happens if no note is brought?

• What are the requirements for pre-arranged absences?

Grading scales and expectations for posting grades. In many cases, grades have become all that matters for some students (and their parents) rather than learning or effort. Make certain all grades you give follow policy guidelines and exemplify the learning of each student. Information to know includes the following:

- Percentage scale for letter grades
- Procedures for recording a standards-based report card, letter grade, or other type of report card used by the school or grade level
- When and how often grades are to be posted and report cards issued
- How contested grades are handled
- How many grades should be posted per day, per week, and per subject

Policies concerning late students. Schools have procedures and policies for students who arrive late at school or class. Be sure you are informed on these and any interventions that are taken.

Policies for accepting makeup work or late work. After a student has been absent, there is often makeup work to complete. As a new teacher, you must have a clear expectation for late work, including possible penalties. Knowing the school or district rules keeps consistency and fairness at the forefront of grading.

Teacher absence procedures. What do you need to do when you have to be absent? Here are some things you need to consider:

- What paperwork must be completed before and after an absence?
- Whom should you notify in case of illness or absence?
- What are acceptable reasons for teacher absences (e.g., family illness, funerals, emergencies)?
- Where should you leave keys, plans for the substitute teacher, the roll book, any confidential information that a substitute must know (e.g., students' allergies, medication schedules)?
- What are the procedures for securing a substitute teacher?

Sick leave and personal leave. To be prepared for planned and unplanned situations in your personal life, it is important to know the answers to questions such as these:

- How many sick days or personal days are allowed each month or year?
- What happens with unused sick leave?
- What happens if you exceed the number of allotted days?

Payroll requirements. When a paycheck arrives, you want to be sure that the deductions are correct and the IRS is happy. Find out the answers to these questions:

- To whom do you report the number of deductions or changes in deductions for the IRS?
- In which IRAs, TSAs, or other retirement plans does the district participate?
- To whom do you report a discrepancy on a payroll receipt?
- Which credit unions and banks does the district have agreements with for automatic deposits or automatic payment of loans?

Personal and family insurance—health, dental, vision. It is important to know about all of the possible deductions and money concerns that are related to your paycheck. Designated personnel are available to help you if you simply ask. Here are some typical questions:

- Is the insurance premium automatically deducted by the payroll department?
- What is the copay cost?
- Are there preferred physicians?

Duty assignments before, during, and after school. As a new teacher, you need to know the duties you will be expected to fulfill, such as bus duty, recess or lunch duty, and hall duty between classes. You are also likely to have "team player" situations, such as being asked to pick up someone else's after-school bus duty or volunteering to chaperone dances.

The school may have other extra duties available, such as coaching, advising clubs, directing plays or concerts, tutoring, or setting up art shows. These activities provide another way to get to know your students on a more personal level as well as to support school events. They also can be very time-consuming, so select extra duties carefully to avoid being overwhelmed. It is easy to get caught up in too many activities and responsibilities. New teachers may fall prey to those who want to hand off their existing duties and jobs. Select activities that you love because of your talents, past experiences, and personal knowledge. When it comes to generating success, few things match enthusiasm and dedication. As a bonus, some extra duties come with a small stipend to supplement your new teacher salary.

Activities after school hours, including parent conferences and athletic, music, and art events. As a new staff member, you need to know the procedures for report card conferences. Sometimes parents attend alone; at other times the student attends with the parents. When students are present, it is beneficial to allow them to share insight about learning and progress being made in the subject areas. It is also critical to stick to a time schedule so that one parent does not dominate your time, leaving other parents waiting or with only a few minutes to visit with you.

Teachers are also required to attend many special events, and often these include specific responsibilities such as collecting money or chaperoning. When teachers attend student events outside the classroom, their presence is appreciated and has a positive effect on students.

Dress codes for students and teachers. What are the rules regarding students' clothing—length of skirts, logos on shirts, flip-flops, belts, or pants with holes? Are there dress-up days? Casual days? What about staff dress codes? You may be able to be a trendsetter by promoting professional attire!

Promotion and graduation requirements for the school, district, and state. Knowing about these requirements is essential, so that when you are planning ahead and determining student strengths and areas of concern, you can make sure that all students achieve the essentials for moving to the next grade level.

Suspected child abuse, neglect, or endangerment. Suspected child abuse, neglect, or endangerment is frightening. As a teacher you have an absolute responsibility to report any suspicion or any bit of evidence suggesting that a child's life is not safe. You cannot ignore the situation or put off reporting until later. Be sure you know to whom, when, and where to report these concerns and the necessary paperwork that must be completed.

Teachers must see, hear, and interact with children with acute sensitivity. Although they cannot always immediately pinpoint what the difference is in a child on a certain day, teachers can observe changes in attitude, in dress, or in behavior. Knowing and understanding every student individually empowers your teaching and benefits and protects students.

Confidentiality. It is important to maintain confidentiality with much of the information gleaned in your classroom and events that happen within your school. Student learning and growth in your classroom are private matters to be shared with colleagues who can help you achieve optimal success with each child or with parents who need to know how to best support their child and her educational development. Gossip in the lounge or idle conversations at the grocery store are inappropriate.

When teachers discuss issues that directly affect a student's learning, the discussion is often referred to as "educational need-to-know," meaning that there is a purpose and desired outcome for learning as classroom information is disclosed. Your goal is always to seek solutions that promote student learning and enhance your teaching skills.

Although I have just mentioned essential information for new teachers, the list is in no way exhaustive. You are now equipped with many of the questions to ask so that you will have the information you need to successfully deal with the business side of a teaching career.

During my first year of teaching physical education, we had just begun our jump rope unit and students were practicing all types of skills with heavy, plastic beaded ropes. After class, as the girls filed into the locker room and then the showers, I noticed horrendous red welts on one student's back. She had had several bruises earlier in the year as a result of falling or bumping into things, but these welts were fresh and terrible. *Oh, no,* I thought, *she has been beaten.*

As I gathered my wits and pondered the report I would need to file, another girl passed by me with similar red welts—and then another and another. I eventually deduced that these welts had come from the jump ropes hitting their backs during practice, not from abuse. Relief flooded over me, but I had been reminded of the enormous responsibility that teachers have for the safety and well-being of every student. On our next jump rope day, we discussed rope safety and I recommended that students wear a sweatshirt when learning or perfecting jump rope skills.

Communication

Although you may not think of communication as part of the business aspect of teaching, it will play an important role in your day-to-day functioning and your eventual success as a teacher. Communication should be part of both your initial preparation and your ongoing activity. From the outset new teachers need to communicate with everyone with whom they work. Great communication builds bridges and improves relationships. Frequent, clear communication is critical to let others know what is taking place in your classroom and to encourage people to come to you with questions instead of guessing or relying on hearsay.

Communication with Students and Parents Before School Begins

Before the bell has rung and the students see their new teacher for the first time, they will be more comfortable if they feel that they know you and will be safe and well taught while they are with you. As soon as the class lists arrive, send a letter to each student. Include some background information about yourself and what students can expect in your classroom. If they will need special supplies for class or projects, include a list in the letter. A friendly note before school starts is appropriate for all students, regardless of age. Students like to have a clear sense of the upcoming year and an overall idea of their new teacher and course expectations.

Written communication with students and parents should continue throughout the coming months, with the goal of sending an individual note of praise to every student by the end of the year. If you write a few letters or postcards each week, the task is not overwhelming. A note of appreciation after students have left for the next grade is another way to personalize teaching. Positive school–home connections create great avenues of communication.

If your school has a monthly newsletter that includes a calendar of events or a section on classroom projects, performances, and upcoming programs, include information about your class. If your school doesn't have a newsletter, begin one for your class or grade level or subject area. A newsletter is a friendly way to foster connections between school and home.

Communication is especially important for any nonroutine school-day events that require advance notice, including special projects and presentations or field trips. The more parents know about what's coming up, the less chance for miscommunication or confusion.

Communication with Administrators, Coworkers, Support Staff, and Others

It is also important to communicate with the other people who work in the building and shape teaching, learning, and student success. When things go perfectly, the administrator wants to know. When a disaster rages, keeping your supervisor in the loop may save many heartaches.

Coworkers, along with all of the support staff in the school, are there to assist you, to listen to you, to answer your many questions, and to offer advice when you need it. Of course, all of the people in the school are not equally willing and able to help a new teacher. Again, seek advice wisely and select ideas to implement carefully. Although most coworkers mean well when they share, new teachers do not want to be swamped with too much "help."

Communication Log

Maintain a record of all communication with colleagues, administrators, students, parents, and volunteers. A communication log like that shown in Figure 2.1 includes a place to quickly jot the date, form of communication (phone message, e-mail, written note), name and identifier (student, parent, administrator, colleague, volunteer), purpose of the communication, and a brief note about the interaction. Keep the log in a notebook for quick and easy reference.

Organized Support Programs

In addition to the day-to-day information and advice you seek and receive from your more experienced colleagues, you may find that organized support is available in your school or district. Two common forms of such support are mentor programs and teachers unions.

Figure 2.1	Communication Log			
Date	Form of Contact (phone, e-mail)	Name	Purpose	Results

Mentor Programs

In many districts, a mentor is assigned shortly after a new teacher is hired. A mentor is a master teacher who supports and guides you during your first years on the job. The responsibilities of a mentor vary from daily hands-on observation and assistance to an occasional breeze-by to see if you are still in the room. Although the former may wear you out with an overwhelming determination to make you the best teacher ever, the intent is to share expert advice so that you can become more proficient.

If a mentor has not been assigned to help, carefully observe your colleagues to discover the professional leader who can best assist you. Somewhere in the school there is a teacher/confidant waiting to support new educators during their first year on the job. You will be able to recognize these excellent teachers by the following indicators:

- Skillful organization of their classrooms
- Cheerful, positive attitude at all times, about every aspect of teaching and being a teacher
- Knowledge and understanding concerning students, learning, lessons, and success for all
- Ability to share ideas and strategies with others while at the same time listening intently to input
- Respect for every administrator, coworker, support staff, and child in the school

By surrounding yourself with excellence, your teaching skills and knowledge will flourish.

Teachers Unions

You can learn about many policies and other district information from union representatives of the school or district. Unions and their work within districts vary greatly, and the acceptance of the union as a positive force varies as well. Check with your mentor or other coworkers to find out more about the role of unions in your district.

Surviving on a Beginning Salary

With your certificate in order and the job about to begin, there is something that you must still be wondering about—payday. Payday often comes four to six weeks into the contract year. Many teachers feel it is necessary to work extra jobs to make ends meet. Realize that it is impossible to teach full-time with absolute dedication and maintain another job. Balancing a budget, counting pennies, and deciding how you can focus your time and energy wisely will strengthen your teaching.

Although schools often supply items such as pencils and paper, crayons and notebooks, you may find yourself paying for many materials necessary for setting up a classroom, such as bulletin board materials, additional teaching supplies, and small rewards for students. In addition, you'll need appropriate clothing for professional dress. It is essential to budget wisely. The new car may have to wait for a year or two.

Closing Advice

Being aware of the business aspects of the job and having open and clear communication with everyone who is part of your school life will alleviate some of the stress and free up time for the actual instruction of students. When you bring the best of yourself to the job—your knowledge, skills, and love of learning—instruction and learning improve every day. Experience really is a wise teacher. It may be challenging as you work to achieve excellence, but the job is also energizing and revitalizing. Teaching is magic. Although teachers do not always witness the results of their work, so much of the lifelong success of every individual comes from the foundation provided by an inspirational, educational expert—a teacher.

3

Standards, Curriculum, and Textbooks

• • •

You've learned about school and district policies, handled all the business details related to the job, and established an organized way to communicate regularly with colleagues, students, parents, and others. Now it is time to enter your new domain, the classroom.

Teaching is an enormous responsibility. To reach and teach every child is incredibly difficult and challenging as well as richly rewarding. To ensure that you are teaching to school, district, and state academic expectations, it is important to study the standards for learning, unite them with the curriculum, and examine the school calendar and pacing guide. Then you need to gather textbooks and other materials and instructional tools and organize your lesson plan book. Preplanning with educational goals in mind sets you and your students up for organized, sequential learning. To know where you are going and then arrive at the learning destination requires finely tuned preparation. Adjustments will be necessary during the year, but you will discover that hours spent in planning lead to classroom success.

The Challenge

I was observing in a 1st grade classroom with a highly skilled teacher, Anna DeVries. Her students were busily engaged with partners, editing and revising their writing. While each pair was deeply engrossed in rich discussion (yes, 1st graders can be gifted writers and excellent at analyzing their work, especially when these activities are part of their daily instruction), Anna moved around the room, advising, overseeing student work, and listening to their conversations.

I listened in on two students, one of whom was struggling with end punctuation. His partner recommended putting a question mark at the end of a sentence, but the uncertain student was reluctant to follow this advice. Finally the partner stood up in frustration, pointed to the writing standards posted on the board, and announced, "Remember, the Nevada State Standard, 'All sentences will end with appropriate punctuation.' A question mark is appropriate here." Because he spoke with authority and true knowledge, his partner nodded and then added a question mark to his work.

Lessons Learned

Students are listening to every word you say. They like knowing what they should be learning and what the goals are for study. Organized lessons that address the learning standards for your grade level or subject area have the highest potential for positive effects on your students, their knowledge, and their understanding.

Weeks Before the First Bell

Shortly after the interview when the job is awarded, teachers receive a set of magical keys. These keys are both literal and metaphoric in what they reveal. The literal keys open the door to the school and classroom every day; the metaphoric keys allow teachers to enter the lives and minds of students. Extraordinary power and responsibility are granted to teachers. The wonders of learning that lie ahead are astounding as the novice grows and develops into a skilled professional.

As you confidently stride into your new room, you should find textbooks, supplementary materials, academic standards, curriculum maps, and pacing charts. If these materials are not in your room, ask for them immediately. These items are necessary for preparation before school begins.

You can hope that your classroom has all of the books and materials that you need. Sometimes, however, the school vultures have swooped in the minute the last teacher vacated the room, stripping it bare. In that case, you will have to search and beg for appropriate teaching tools. On the other hand, the previous teacher may have retired and left you with every book, paper, activity, and teaching item used since the beginning of education. Now you must sort and sift to find the items that meet your teaching needs and discard the rest.

Becoming Familiar with Academic Standards

Long before the first students peek in the door, teachers have much to do, beginning with laying out a format for the year's learning, including lessons based on academic standards. Well-formulated lessons incorporating standards are the foundation of instruction. Understanding the standards and designing lessons to meet them are time-consuming and complex tasks, so the sooner you begin, the better prepared you will be for excellent instruction. With standards-based lessons in mind, examine the adopted textbooks and other supplementary materials that are available to develop a picture of the year of learning ahead.

In the past, many teachers "tornadoed" into teaching with a book in one hand and a vague outline of how to get the job done in the other. Over time, they did figure out what their students needed to know and be able to do. Now district and state academic standards create a learning framework to scaffold instruction, so much of the mystery of what to teach and in what order has been eliminated. The challenge is fitting everything within the allotted time and presenting it in a way that results in students actually learning.

District and State Standards

Why standards? One reason that academic standards are essential is that families move. Because some students may be in as many as five or six different schools during one school year, continuity in academic expectations and what they are taught is critical to their learning and success. Many students struggle with disconnected instruction that results from attending schools without overall plans for what students must know and be able to do at each grade level and in each subject.

In the past teachers were divided by classroom, grade level, and subject area. Teachers taught and students learned many things, but much of education was not planned comprehensively. For example, the dinosaur unit may have been taught in several grades, whereas amphibians were entirely omitted from instruction. Standards provide continuity across grade levels and clarity within subject areas—delineating, for example, the knowledge and skills to be covered in algebra I compared with advanced math, or in beginning word processing compared with computer programming.

With academic standards as the blueprints for instruction, teachers know what students at each grade level and in each subject area need to know and be able to do to be proficient by the end of the term. Elementary school teachers are responsible for grade-level standards in every academic subject that is explicitly taught: language arts, reading, mathematics, science, and social studies. Being prepared requires large amounts of time for reading and interpreting the intent of each standard and then matching instruction to the standard. Although the sheer number of subjects and standards may be overwhelming, a solid understanding of the implications of both subjects and standards ensures readiness to teach with maximum efficiency long before students arrive. Knowing where instruction is headed and planning how to reach your destination are essential to the success of the first year of teaching and to all student learning.

Secondary teachers may have fewer subject areas and standards to study, but that does not mean the job is easier. The expectations for learning increase in difficulty and required output and performance. Teachers must have strong content and background knowledge to design high-quality lessons that reach all learners. For students who move frequently or fall behind for other reasons, each year of school increases the probable need for extensive review, reteaching, and modified instruction to fill in the holes of missed learning. Teachers using academic guidelines based on the standards extend the bridge of current learning and provide support for future learning.

Academic standards documents are available at most school sites, from the school district office, or from the Web site of each individual state department of education. Most standards documents are large and are a lengthy download and printing project, but having the documents is necessary for successful implementation of standards-based instruction.

Copying only the standards related to your grade level or subject area is insufficient. Although your focus is on specific grade-level and subject-area standards, it is essential to also be familiar with the standards taught to students before they arrived at a particular grade or subject and what they need to know and be able to do to succeed at the next level. An overall understanding of the standards means every teacher knows what students have been taught (and hopefully learned) as well as what comes next.

The total vision of learning from kindergarten through senior year in high school reveals the importance of each educational step. You cannot teach in seclusion but, rather, must teach with a vision of teaching such as the one created with the graphic in Chapter 1 (see Figure 1.1, p. 12). Being familiar with other grade-level academic standards helps you determine missing or insufficient attainment of skills and concepts. You can use this insight to develop additional lessons for struggling students as well as to create challenging assignments for students who have met proficiency. Standards are critical to organized, sequential teaching and learning.

Creating Standards Note Cards

As the blueprints for instruction, standards identify concepts and skills that must be taught and the educational expectations of each subject or grade level. You must study them, memorize them, know what comes before and what comes next, and use the standards to create high-quality instruction that integrates learning and prepares students for the future. Figure 3.1 is a step-by-step guide to creating note cards that can help in the effort to become thoroughly familiar with the standards.

Figure 3.1	**Creating Standards Note Cards**

1. Obtain a copy of the standards for your grade level or subject area.

2. Make a copy for your lesson plan book and one to cut up for handy reference.

3. Read through the standards, making notes to yourself about their meaning and implications. If necessary, ask for clarification from colleagues.

4. Purchase some note cards. You may want to color-code these by standard content or concept strand.

5. Cut out one standard per card and paste it on the card.

6. While you are separating your grade-level standards, do not forget that you must also know what comes before your grade and what comes after—the big picture of instruction and learning. Paste the "before" and "after" standards on separate pieces of construction paper for easy reference.

7. When all standards are on cards, punch a hole in the left-hand corner of each card and place the cards on a ring.

8. Note on the back of each card when you will be teaching this standard and ideas for instruction.

9. As you teach, add notes about appropriate exercises, page numbers in your textbook, difficulties encountered, and other helpful information.

10. Place a checkmark and a brief note on each card after you teach or review a standard to remind you of how often you have worked with a particular standard and how your students are progressing.

11. Review previous learning as you add new learning.

District Curriculum Mandates

District curriculum mandates are usually in place for each grade level or subject area. The district curriculum uses the state standards and expands them into district expectations for learning and achievement. It includes more specific information for concepts and skills to be taught and recommendations for instruction. There may also be activities and strategies for classroom use as well as references and resources that provide additional instructional support. The curriculum should match the state academic standards.

Some may say that examining standards is busywork and non-productive. In the many years that I have spent working with teachers and academic standards, I have found that knowing the teaching expectations of subject areas and grade levels has proven to be extremely beneficial to coordinated, meaningful instruction. Not only do teachers better understand the educational requirements, they clearly know what must be taught to help students become proficient.

Teacher's Edition and Supplementary Material

With an understanding of the importance of coordinating lessons with the state and district standards and the district curriculum, it is now time to gather needed materials to teach each lesson (see Chapter 7 for guidance on how to create lesson and unit plans). The teacher's edition of the district-adopted textbook and supplementary materials can guide you in the many steps of planning. Textbooks and materials have been selected by a textbook committee because they are believed to be closely aligned with the state standards and the achievement expectations of the school, the district, and the state. They contain vital material, teaching strategies, instructional ideas, and background information to support good instruction.

As you become familiar with textbooks, you can highlight the many guidelines, suggestions, lessons and minilessons, and recommendations for teaching provided in them. You can compare the concepts and skills presented in the book with the academic standards and grade-level/subject-area expectations. Penciled-in notes, bookmarks, and sticky-note reminders can identify the academic standards that are addressed in each chapter and section of the book. This focused review increases your knowledge of the organizational format of the text and how it relates to meeting key learning goals. For any academic standards that are omitted from the textbook or where explanation and practice are incomplete, you can turn to supplementary materials and other resources to complete your instruction.

Textbooks are excellent tools, but it is improbable that you will start on the first page and then work through the book to meet all learning goals. Being familiar with the textbook layout and features allows you to be selective as you match lessons to the standards.

In general, newer textbooks are designed to facilitate good instruction by being fairly complete, with easy-to-follow guidelines that match learning requirements. They contain formats and activities that are clearly described and simple to implement. How each lesson unfolds depends on your creativity, ingenuity, and knowledge about what students must know and how to best support learning.

I spent time as a facilitator for the Northeast Nevada Math Project, a collaborative venture among the University of Nevada, the Nevada Department of Education, the Northeastern Nevada Regional Professional Development Program, and rural elementary school math teachers. One of my duties included administering the pre- and post-mathematics exams to students in each of the classrooms of participating teachers.

The tests, based on state mathematics standards, were designed to assess past and current learning and to uncover how students solve mathematical problems that contain concepts or skills that they have not yet encountered. Thus 3rd graders had multiplication problems (a 3rd grade academic standard) as well as division problems (a 4th grade academic standard). Students were encouraged to draw, label, explain, and attack each problem with any method they felt would work and to demonstrate how they solved the problem through writing and illustrations.

One 3rd grade student struggled with the problem "91 divided by 4," and he raised his hand to ask for help. "We haven't learned this yet, and I do not know what to do," he said. I responded, "If you thought you knew how to solve this problem, what would you do?"

With this suggestion, his face lit up as he grabbed his pencil and began to draw, circle, make notes, and decode until he cracked the problem and came up with the answer of "22 with 3 'leftovers,'" as he called them. He used his current knowledge to solve an unfamiliar problem.

I started using those words often when students asked me for help: "If you thought you knew how to solve this problem, what would you do?" It is remarkable how this unleashes confidence and competence in students.

Which Comes First: Standards or Textbooks?

From the order of topics in this chapter, the certain response is "The standards!" The standards outline for teachers what students must know and be able to do to become proficient. The teacher then designs instruction that facilitates the desired learning.

Lessons and lesson plans based on the standards can be viewed as the roads, and the textbook and other supplementary material represent various guidebooks that help teachers and students gain knowledge and understanding about the destination. Standards alone are words; chapters in textbooks are more words. Teachers need both for the best and most comprehensive instruction. Study the standards and know the expectations for each; then find the materials that support and extend the learning.

Lesson Plan Book

The lesson plan book is the outline of instruction for the year. You have just so many days and weeks to accomplish it all: teaching the required standards, following the curriculum, assessing and reteaching as necessary, and preparing students for the next level. The lesson plan book is a minute-by-minute, hour-by-hour, daily, weekly, and monthly guide that supports the vision of teaching discussed in Chapter 1. Although you will need to adjust the lesson plan book occasionally, time and practice will make the lessons easier to implement within the allotted time.

You may be a part of a teaching team that has already outlined plans for the year and that can assist you as you create your own classroom plan. If you must go it alone, begin by doing the following:

• Create an overall view of each week of instruction for every class that will be taught during the semester or year.

• Plan a daily overview of instruction for each class. Chapter 7 contains information on lesson plans, including the phases of the lesson and allotting minutes to each phase.

• Determine the standards to be taught and when, and align them with achievement expectations.

• Sequence the standards in a logical, instructional order so they can be used as building blocks of learning throughout the year; standards are not taught, assessed, and then set aside but, rather, integrated again and again into learning.

• Decide the type of assessment that best indicates the degree of proficiency of students.

• Select the overarching learning goals and objectives by day, by week, and for the entire year.

• Study the organizational format of the textbook and how each element enriches lessons and learning.

- Organize supplementary materials to incorporate into learning.
- Plan ways to teach the diverse learners in the classroom.
- Arrange instruction around holidays and special occasions that affect classroom instructional time.
- Think about student pullouts (when all students have other classes such as band or P.E.) and how to transition students in and out.
- Consider additional student pullouts that affect just a few students. How will these students know about all of the crucial learning, announcements, projects, and other information if they are gone?
- Incorporate assessment feedback into future instruction. What have students learned? What needs review or reteaching?
- Reserve an area for special notes about lessons, student learning, ideas for improvement, and the on-the-spot reflections that improve future teaching.

Wow! This task is enormous and difficult when a clear picture of the first year is still intangible. Again, the ultimate goal is to support the big vision of teaching you developed in Chapter 1, and that cannot be created without hard work, forethought, and planning. Begin with one step at a time to outline the year. This picture of the year in the lesson plan book is essential to year-long organization.

Pacing Charts: Timing for Best Results

A pacing chart is the calendar for teaching each standard based on the number of hours of instruction in the day, week, and year. In addition, a pacing chart includes critical dates such as deadlines for when certain standards must be taught so that students are prepared for the next steps of learning and for assessment.

Colleagues may have pacing charts they have used that are available to share. If your school doesn't have a pacing chart, use Figure 3.2 to create your own guide. With the pacing guide, you

Figure 3.2	Creating a Pacing Chart

1. Gather the standards cards that you created in Figure 3.1 and a large piece of poster paper four or five feet long. (Alternatively, tape several sheets of plain white paper together—one for each month of teaching—to create one long sheet.)

2. Divide the poster paper into the number of months of instruction for your school.

3. Write the name of each month across the top of the paper, beginning with your first month of school and ending with your last month, stretching the year across the paper.

4. Divide each month into weeks (days may be added later).

5. Note the number of holidays and noninstructional days for each month.

6. Note key testing dates (national tests, state tests) and circle them, marking them as dates for meeting instructional goals. (If state testing is in March, waiting until April to instruct students on key concepts deprives them of some of the necessary learning tools for achievement.)

7. Place each standard card in the appropriate month, in what you believe to be a sequence that will help you achieve your teaching goals for the year.

8. By looking at the month, determine what standards you will emphasize each week.

9. Draw lines across the months in which you believe you will need additional instruction or review, or for topics that do not end. For example, when you teach the scientific method, you do not teach it once and then move on. Instead you incorporate the scientific method into all inquiry throughout the year, from August through June. The standard remains the same, but the degree of proficiency increases.

10. Once you are satisfied with your layout, write the standard or the key words of the standard as reference.

now have a big picture for the year. Plan to review and update your pacing chart often. Use large sheets of paper so you can add extra notes, mark standards that need repeating, or add insights for standards that need practice and review. Although computers are wonderful tools that simplify our lives, I have found that physical manipulation of the note cards (see Figure 3.1, p. 37) and the pieces of the pacing chart invites intense discussion and interaction with grade-level and subject-area colleagues. A large visual chart benefits students as they track their progress.

Well-planned instruction to reach learning goals begins on day one and ends on the last day of school. Careful planning enables teachers to accomplish far more because they clearly know the requirements for learning and have a plan for achieving all of them. The pacing chart encompasses all that needs to be accomplished within the allotted number of school days and is part of the road map to success.

The pacing chart is a living document and is part of all pre- and postplanning. Preplanning is charting the course of instruction; postplanning is analyzing how the lesson has gone, where students are now, and what you must do next to ensure that all students have the opportunity to succeed. Pacing an entire year is an enormous challenge, but the knowledge gained guides and supports instruction.

As mentioned earlier, teaching involves much more than standards. Individual personal touches and the love of learning and teaching are part of the mix. Your devotion and enthusiasm will motivate and inspire students.

Closing Advice

Just as a carpenter cannot construct a home without a solid, well-formulated plan, foundation, framework, and materials, an excellent teacher cannot begin teaching and expect outstanding results without hours and days and weeks of planning. For teachers hired two days before school starts, there are some 48-hour days ahead!

Knowing the standards, learning the curriculum, studying the textbook and supplemental materials, organizing the lesson plan book, and establishing a pacing chart are extremely valuable activities. Preparing to teach is sometimes as exhausting as the actual instruction, but all the effort contributes to success. During the first year of teaching, your confidence level will alternate between feeling as though you're gliding through the water like an Olympic swimmer and feeling as if you are being sucked under by a whirlpool of demands. Just remember, each year of teaching and practice will increase your capability and self-confidence.

4

Classroom Management

• • •

In Chapter 3 you learned that setting goals and determining how to reach them is essential groundwork for your first year of teaching. Steps include making sure you understand state and district academic standards, becoming thoroughly familiar with the district curriculum, scrutinizing the teacher's edition of textbooks and supplementary materials, and organizing a lesson plan book that includes instructional pacing.

Now it is time to design a classroom management plan with two major elements: (1) rules that maintain discipline and allow students to learn, and (2) consequences that support the rules. You cannot teach and few students can learn if all students do not believe that the rules for behavior apply to them. By establishing clear expectations from the outset, coupled with consequences that address and quickly eliminate problems, you and your students will thrive. Students want well-organized instruction and a fair teacher who enforces the rules with everyone. Clarify your behavior plan and then follow through with impartial justice. Classroom management is key to skilled teaching and enhances learning by optimizing time on task.

The Challenge

In 6th grade I had my first male teachers, Mr. Holmes and Mr. Fuston. These two men were inspirational, wise, and wonderful at clear instruction, and we all loved them. Occasionally my friend Teresa and I would beg Mr. Fuston to let us stay in at lunch, especially when it was cold outside. On this particular day, the wind was howling, snow was blowing, and staying in was a reasonable request.

After we finished eating we decided that it would be really fun to race around the room, leaping from desk to desk without touching the floor. Our goal was to see how many laps we could make before someone fell. It seemed like an interesting game, and we never considered that it might be inappropriate. On about our seventh lap, Mr. Fuston stepped into the room and in a deep, rumbling voice said, "I am so disappointed! Get down, get out, and be ready for your detention!"

Teresa and I grabbed our coats and slunk out the door, choking back tears, shivering with fear. First of all, we had never heard Mr. Fuston raise his voice before, so that shocked us. Further, we had been threatened with *detention*! Oh, no! Not detention! We were in for it now.

Then as one we said, "Detention? I wonder what that means?" As the reentry bell rang, we tiptoed into the room, shaking little frostbitten urchins. We slipped silently into our desks and waited for *it* to happen: detention.

Lessons went on, and we worked diligently until dismissal, with Mr. Fuston never uttering another word to us. After a sleepless night we returned to school the following day, waiting for detention to slap us in the face. Shortly after the bell rang, Teresa and I tried to slip inconspicuously into our seats. Soon, however, we were called to Mr. Fuston's desk. Detention included cleaning desks at recess for two weeks and not being allowed in the classroom unless our teacher was present. Although the punishment may not seem huge, knowing that we had disappointed our teacher weighed on us for the rest of the year.

Lessons Learned

Your students will interpret your words in various ways. The way you act and react along with the way you make students feel have a lasting effect on them. In the scenario with Mr. Fuston, the detention was minimal when compared with letting him down through our inappropriate behavior. We learned to be more respectful in the classroom as we worked to regain our teacher's trust. Respect and trust are essential to your relationships with students, colleagues—truly, with everyone.

Establishing Rules That Work

It is essential to develop basic classroom rules before students arrive. The rules must pinpoint expectations for students, including exactly how you visualize appropriate behavior. Students need to recognize teacher leadership from the moment they enter the room. Unclear or nonexistent rules invite challenge from some students, who may view their new teacher as weak or disorganized. Good rules that are clearly explained and are understood by students set you up as a savvy expert. Rules also free the classroom from disruption so that you can teach and your students can learn.

Imagine the rules that will make your classroom operate smoothly. The goal of rules is to create an atmosphere that is conducive to learning. To help you determine what rules your classroom will need, brainstorm ideas for each of these prompts:

- Appropriate behavior in my classroom will look like ...
- Appropriate behavior in my classroom will sound like ...
- Appropriate behavior in my classroom will feel like ...
- I will know my students are on task and learning because ...

Some teachers and students like bustling action and noise; others can cope with few distractions of any sort. All students need a classroom that feels welcoming and safe and that offers a rich learning environment.

Because the goal is to have students learn, concentrate on how behavior affects student learning. Good rules focus on the respect that students have for their teacher and for the other students in the classroom. Respect also includes how the teacher treats students. Sometimes, especially early in a teaching career, new teachers put more emphasis on being liked by their students than being respected by them. It is helpful if students like you, but their respect for their teacher is what really makes the difference. Your job is teaching students, not being a buddy.

The majority of your students will care about you. When they make mistakes, most often it is because they did not think wisely or they simply made a poor decision—they are children after all. When a rule is broken, it fractures trust, but that does not mean that the situation cannot heal. By being alert to possible problems before they can happen, you will prevent many of them. When you deal with the situation swiftly and with relative calm, following the already delineated consequences, teaching and peace can resume with the focus on good instruction, not misbehavior and distractions.

Students learn from everything their teachers say or do and the example of respect that has been established. With high standards for behavior launched the first day and maintained throughout the year, the focus is on good instruction and learning.

Basic Classroom Rules

Here are essential rules to include in your classroom management plan:

- Be on time, seated, and prepared with all materials required for learning.
- Be polite and courteous to all class members and the teacher.
- Turn in all work complete and on time in the appropriate place, with name, date, and period written on it.
- Obey all school rules concerning behavior and dress.

These rules cover the primary requirements for any smoothly running classroom. They are positive in nature, and each promotes an atmosphere for learning. Add rules to the list if necessary, but do not overwhelm yourself or your students with micromanagement. What is most important is that clear rules are established, practiced, and adhered to from the outset.

Although the rules are effective with any age group, they may require different degrees of explanation and practice. Most secondary students are fully familiar with the list. A short discussion of your expectations should suffice. Elementary students need specific guidance about the expectations and may require extensive practice. This does not mean repeating the rule over and over again but, rather, clarifying it, practicing it, and then adhering to it consistently.

For example, because courtesy includes listening attentively without side conversations, teachers must never find themselves talking over their students. From the first day, establish a quiet signal such as raising a hand and then waiting for silence from students before continuing, or counting down "5, 4, 3, 2, 1," with silence expected by the time you reach 1. Require the same respect whenever students speak as well. Again, teachers cannot teach and students cannot learn when behavior problems are disrupting the classroom.

You've Established the Rules, but What Do They Mean?

In the detention story, Teresa and I did not know what "detention" meant, but we did respect Mr. Fuston so much that we altered our behavior immediately to please him. Not all students are quite that eager to please, so be prepared to enforce classroom rules while remembering that students make mistakes. You want respectful observance of rules, not a battle over the purpose of the rules.

It is important to know your definition of each of the rules and exactly what you expect for student behavior. What is "courteous"? Some of your students may come from homes where courtesy means less loud yelling and hitting. What does it mean to be "on time, seated, and prepared"? What is your vision of these? Does "on time" mean zipping in the door as the bell sounds? In the room but not seated? Near the seat but not quite in it? Or falling into the seat before the bell completes its final tone? Determining the definition of "on time" and the expectations for it and then deciding how to clearly explain and enforce the rule will result in a rule that works. Warning after warning is ineffective. Consistent enforcement maintains control even though that requires never-ending vigilance.

Consistent enforcement involves clear communication with students, so that they understand the consequences for breaking the rules. If you define "on time" as completely in the desk as the bell sounds, how will you handle a late student who is not quite there? Discussion or argument with a student while trying to begin class accomplishes nothing but frustration. With late students, you must first recognize that students are late for a variety of valid and invalid reasons. Because you have already stated and explained the rules and expectations (to be on time, seated, and ready to work), the late student now follows the procedure for violating this rule. The student is obviously late; no words are needed. (See the section Consequences for Breaking Rules later in this chapter.)

● ● ● ● ● ● ● ●

Finally, you must realize that your individual classroom management plan resides within the larger school environment. What if the rules for tardiness and dress code are poorly enforced throughout the school, so that you feel you are the only one enforcing them? Troubleshooting potential problems with dozens of "What ifs?" can help you anticipate challenges and avoid difficulties.

Procedure for Dealing with Tardy Students

The first part of the first basic rule involves being on time, and so developing a clear procedure for handling tardy students should be one of the main elements of your classroom management plan. The procedure described here works well. The tardy student will

- Quietly enter the classroom.
- Write his name on the board in the designated spot for later reference; this procedure applies to both excused and unexcused tardies to save further interruption.
- Retrieve a Late Pass note (Figure 4.1, p. 52) from a predefined location and complete it.
- Staple any passes or notes from the office or another teacher or parent to the Late Pass note (if this applies) for reference.

You can discuss the Late Pass note with the student later, as necessary; sometimes the note solves the problem, but at other times, intervention is needed. Retain the copy in your Behavior Log or Late Pass files for reference.

An excused tardy becomes a nonissue, unless the tardiness occurs frequently and interferes with learning. An unexcused tardy is explained on the Late Pass note. Thus the cause of being late becomes the focus rather than the disruption of being late. Although excused and unexcused tardies require different actions on your part, neither must interrupt the other students' learning. If tardy students know precisely what to do when they are late, they are not disruptive. You are now free to continue instruction and to deal with the issue at a more convenient time.

With younger students who are often late, set up a conference with the person who brings the child to school to find out why the child does not arrive on time. Chronic lateness is a problem that needs resolution so that the child does not miss critical instruction.

Figure 4.1	Sample Late Pass

Student's Name:

Date:

Brief explanation for late arrival:

Signature of student:

Please leave this note in the Late Pass box on the teacher's desk.

Teacher response and notes:

_____ Excused   _____ Unexcused

_____ We will discuss this at the end of the period.

On Time, Prepared

The first basic rule also includes being prepared. What exactly does that mean? Does it mean that students arrive with the proper books, notebooks, and other learning utensils? The majority of students come prepared every day, but you must decide what to do with students who frequently forget to bring learning materials with them. What will you do when a student has none of the following items?

- Book
- Notebook
- Paper
- Pencil, pen, colored pencils
- Assignment
- Special materials (such as cloth for sewing, poster board for presentation, protractor for math)

Deciding how to handle each situation before it occurs means never being caught at a loss as to how to solve it. Remember, instructional goals are to teach and have students learn, not to argue over pencils and books.

I have recently witnessed what I consider a bothersome trend. To avoid confrontation with students about materials in class, the teacher (especially at the secondary level) provides everything every day—pencils, paper, rulers, and the textbook, which is retrieved for class and then chucked into the corner after class as the student leaves the room. I realize teachers must pick their battles with students and materials, but to expect no responsibility from students begets further irresponsibility.

The more organized and specific you are in terms of expectations for the start of class, the easier the rules are to enforce. When the rules are clear and operational, they become automatic, and class begins with ease.

After thinking extensively about the first rule—on time, seated, and prepared—complete your own version of Figure 4.2, p. 54. Brainstorm additional ideas on how to make all rules work. For example, to make sure students understand what "Be polite and courteous" means, you could have students role-play appropriate and inappropriate behavior.

Again, when you have determined exactly what behavior you expect of students and the students understand your expectations, worries about classroom management decline. Recognize that you may have to modify or clarify the rule when it is not working. If change or clarification is necessary, act immediately, not next week or next year. It is not easy to adjust classroom rules midyear, but misbehavior cannot continue.

Establishing classroom rules for student behavior is one of the most important things to do on the first day of class. Students who behave are students who can be engaged in learning. Although some teachers create their rules with input from students, I believe that time is far better spent communicating your predetermined rules and expectations for behavior rather than holding a classwide discussion.

Again, young students who are new to school need more practice and reminders about appropriate behavior. Some students

Figure 4.2	Rules and Consequences Preparation Guide
Classroom Rules	**Set Consequences for Breaking These Common Rules**
• **Be on time, seated, and ready to learn.**	• Dashing in the door as the bell sounds • Noisy entry into class that disrupts instruction
• **Be prepared with all materials required for learning.** This rule is especially pertinent for secondary students who have lockers and backpacks.	• Broken pencils or dry pens • Missing notebooks, books, paper, project materials
• **Be polite and courteous.** What does being polite and courteous look like? Sound like? Respect for the teacher, self, and peers is a necessity.	• Blurting answers • Giving inappropriate responses • Disrupting class • Showing disrespect • Stealing, lying • Cheating
• **Turn in all work complete and on time.** This rule is critical to teaching and learning for all students. Dealing with problems in this area can overwhelm teachers without preplanning.	• Turning in work after deadline or during instruction • Handing in makeup work beyond grace period

may not have any idea of what appropriate school behavior really is. They will probably know even less about following procedures and schedules (covered in Chapter 6).

At the secondary level, where teachers may have more than 200 students, it is essential that each student know and understand the classroom rules. Rules cannot be vague or inconsistent. Situations in which teachers are yelling madly or exhibiting extreme frustration with certain students often reflect wobbly rules. In such situations the teacher must regroup and take charge completely. When the teacher feels angry with students because of their behavior, classroom management can be restored by reviewing the rules, considering what might be aggravating the problem, and determining how to make the rules work better.

Some students may want to manipulate the rules, especially when they feel too comfortable. Here the importance of the concept of students who like their teacher versus students who respect their teacher becomes clear. It is nice when students like their teacher because it makes the teacher feel good, but it is critical that they respect their teacher.

Reminders About Classroom Rules

Putting together a classroom management plan involves this handful of essentials:

- You know the rules.
- You are willing to enforce each rule all of the time.
- Your consequences for breaking a rule match the "crime."

There is a huge difference between being late to class, chewing gum, using profanity, and fighting. You want things under control, but you do not need to be a control freak. Injuring oneself or others is not like putting a paper in the wrong basket. By weighing expectations and consequences carefully—perhaps several times over—you can be certain that you are being fair to all. Figure 4.2 can help you determine how you will enforce the rules you establish. It is sometimes difficult to determine how to enforce rules until you are on the job, but planning can help circumvent potential problems.

Good rules mean you are free to lead the instruction, discussion, and activities that best help students learn. Students cannot learn and excel if chaos reigns. On the other hand, good behavior by students increases time for learning. Planning the rules and management goals before school begins is well worth the time and effort.

Remember, ignored misbehavior rarely disappears. Attending to it leads to consistent classroom management. For students who cannot adhere to classroom rules, even when those rules have been explained and practiced, you may need an individual behavior modification plan. The school counselor or resource

Figure 4.3	Behavior Log		
Date	Student's Name	Rule Infraction	Action(s) Taken

teachers can help you establish rules that help each student succeed.

Be aware that all classroom rules are adjusted or overridden when bodily fluids—blood, vomit, excessive tears—are involved or under any emergency medical conditions. These situations demand instantaneous attention and definitely change the flow of instruction. Follow your school's prescribed method for accessing help. Safety for yourself and all your students is imperative.

A Warning About Change and Behavior

Things happen and life changes. Although you may have established excellent rules, discussed them, explained them, practiced them, and then enforced them every day with students, events can transform reality. If one day the classroom atmosphere suddenly feels different, identify the cause and then adjust the rules as needed. These environmental conditions might include the following:

• **Changes in barometric pressure.** Although this may sound crazy, approaching storms, windy days, snow, beautiful spring sunshine, and similar weather events can change the conditions for learning with your students.

• **New students joining the class.** Who knows what rules and expectations they bring with them?

• **Students who leave the classroom.** Whether they were perfectly behaved or slightly less than perfectly behaved, classroom dynamics alter.

- **Vacations.** Although a holiday is delightful for most students, for others it is a lonely, sad time. There may be family fighting, unwanted visitors in the home, too much time alone while parents work, or worse.
- **You, the teacher.** Some days you may not feel well, you may be dealing with distress, or you may just have other anxieties overtaking your brain. Students sense this, and, usually, they worry. Disguise distractions as best as possible, but remember that students who love and care about their teacher (and most of them do) will be disturbed when you are not quite yourself.
- **Each individual student.** Students come to school with complicated lives. Many are dealing with adult issues even though they are just children. Teaching also requires some mind-reading to figure out what is happening with each child.

Share your rules with a mentor or with coworkers to receive their insightful feedback based on experience. By planning ahead and troubleshooting possible problems, prepared teachers are able to circumvent many difficulties.

My 7th grade language arts teacher, Mr. Vick, ruled by fear and threat. He would swoop around the room glaring at each of us. We learned from him, but it was survival learning, not inspired learning. At Christmas he created a red and green ditto sheet for a test. As silly 7th graders, we all laughed as he handed it out. "Way to get into the Christmas spirit, Mr. Vick!" was shouted up and down the rows.

With brow furrowed and eyes glaring, he screeched, "Who said that? Who said that?" Realizing the idiocy of our blurting sarcasm, we all hunkered low in our desks, each hoping that his victim would be somebody else. As he whirled in rage his eyes landed on me. He raised his red and green papers in the air and prepared to swat my head with them as he screamed, "Was it you? Was it you?"

I crouched lower. His fury suddenly subsided, and he went to the front of the room and then thrust the test at us in silence. I was so frightened that I could barely get myself through the test and out the door when the bell finally rang. Thinking that the entire event was my fault, I never spoke a word about this to my parents or to my friends. I simply tried to get through the year as invisible as possible.

Mr. Vick's reign of terror was deadly to learning, to spirit, to curiosity, and to the innocent joking of young adolescents. Had I not had many other wonderful teachers during my school years, I cannot imagine that I would have selected a career in education.

Who Inspired You to Become a Teacher?

Mr. Vick did inspire me to never treat others as he had treated us. On the positive side, it was the kind, caring, and motivational teachers who loved their grade level or subject, loved to learn, and loved each student who have made a difference.

Think of a teacher who motivated you to learn, to develop your skills, and perhaps even to become a teacher. This person has had a powerful influence on you. Most likely you were further inspired by the way that the teacher conducted classes and the positive attitude and respectful behavior that were always exemplified. As you reflect on this individual, answer the following questions:

- What were this teacher's inspiring attributes?
- How did this teacher motivate and inspire you to learn?
- How did this inspirational teacher get the job of teaching done? What classroom management techniques were used?
- How did this teacher reward students for learning?

Consider how you can weave these attributes, motivational techniques, classroom rules, management style, and rewards for learning into your own teaching and expectations for students. The traits that you admire in another teacher are often characteristics that you already possess and that you will bring to your classroom. Imagine how many students will work to gain your caring respect so they can be just like you when they grow up!

Consequences for Breaking Rules

Students who respect their teachers want to please them and to learn from them. Some students, however, may feel compelled to challenge the classroom management plan, especially if they sense their teacher is unwilling or unable to enforce the rules. Breaking rules then becomes a game. To avoid this situation, you must supplement good rules with a plan of action for reasonable sequential consequences when students do not behave properly.

As much as possible, you will want to handle classroom management without outside help (other teachers or the office). By doing this, students develop respect for you as they recognize that you are on top of the game and farsighted in planning. If students sense inconsistency or think that you are distracted or unaware of classroom happenings, problems may then arise.

Think of breaking rules as a small hole in your favorite sweatshirt. The hole represents your students who break rules; the sweatshirt is the rule. You can ignore the hole, but it won't go away. After washing the sweatshirt and ignoring the hole several times, the hole will get bigger, and often inexplicably, more holes will develop.

If, however, at the first hint of a problem you address it and patch it, your sweatshirt may last for years. Know your rules. Know your consequences. Stitch the holes in both of these before they can spread and multiply. A little repair early on means you and your sweatshirt (and teaching career) will last a long time.

With the rules outlined, you now must determine the consequences for breaking them. What are the exact steps to be followed to accomplish a classroom management goal? Here is a suggested consequence plan you can use as a guide.

First sign of a problem—warning.

• A warning may be eliminated once you are sure that students know and understand the rules. It is pointless to warn students day after day. They should already know the rules and expectations.

Step 1: Rule is broken—name written on board.

* Write the student's name on the board as a reminder to yourself and to the student that a rule has been broken.

Step 2: Rule is broken again—check mark by name on the board and detention.

* Place a check mark by the student's name on the board. The student knows that her name with a check mark means loss of a privilege. She loses part of recess or lunchtime—something of value to the student. Quickly and quietly move the student away from the problem.

Step 3: Rule is broken a third time—another check mark and additional detention.

* Place a second check mark by the student's name. Two check marks indicate a longer period of time taken from the student to work on behavior; this time may include in-class or in-school detention.

Step 4: Rule is broken again—call home.

* Place a third check mark by the student's name.
* Make a phone call to the student's home, preferably with the student present. If possible, call home immediately; however, do not let the call interrupt teaching other students. Also avoid calling parents at work unless you have permission to do so. The student may join in the conversation, depending on her attitude and if you believe that this will remedy the behavior issue. Students most often recognize and admit poor behavior when they also respect their teacher. The goal is for you, the student, and the parents or guardians to agree on a solution to resolve the behavior. Do not be surprised, however, if the parents do not follow through with the backup plan. Often misbehavior at school

reflects lack of control at home. The parents may even ask you for help.

- If you do not feel a phone call has resolved the difficulty, request that a counselor, administrator, or other school official schedule a parent-student-teacher conference. If none of the school personnel can attend, ask a trusted colleague to join the conference as a precautionary support. This person provides an extra set of eyes and ears but should not speak or offer advice during the conference. You may ask for feedback from this colleague after the conference, but as the regular classroom teacher, you must exert authority with the parents and student during the conference. Make this noninterference clear to the invited peer before the conference. You must be recognized by the student and parents as the person in charge.

- Have the student attend at least part of the conference so she knows what is being discussed. The conference is not secret sabotage but an effort to solve a disciplinary problem.

Step 5: Rule is broken again—outside intervention.

- As a last resort, send the student to the appropriate administrator with a written referral. An office trip should be reserved for repeated misbehavior, when you feel that the situation can be remedied in no other way, or when the incident is dangerous or threatening. Do not argue or debate with the student. If the student refuses to go, call for help immediately.

- If school policy requires a written report when students are sent to the office, write a report promptly. It is also important to meet with an administrator later to discuss the incident and to learn how the situation is being handled and any expectations for follow-up.

- If at the end of the conference with the parent or administrator you feel as if you are in more trouble than the student, it is obvious that you need to seriously reconsider how to enforce your classroom management plan, knowing that outside support will be minimal.

Any student who repeatedly misbehaves in a period or day is creating a management nightmare. This is why the problem must be solved immediately. Most often the first few steps—writing the name on the board and adding a check mark, along with a short talk about expectations—resolve the problem. One great benefit of a consequence plan is that the teacher and the students already know what will happen after any misbehavior occurs, thus eliminating surprises and blowups.

Here is one important caveat: When student behavior is deemed dangerous to you, to other students, or to the student himself, skip the steps and call for help immediately.

A Fresh Start for Each Period and Each Day

Remember that every day starts fresh. Anger, misunderstanding, or thoughts of reprisal cannot carry over. If students feel like they are prejudged before entering the classroom each day, there is little chance their behavior will improve. A smile, a friendly greeting, and an engaging start to class are ways of letting students know that you do not carry a grudge.

Using the suggestions presented here, think about the consequences and behavior plan that will work for you. Ideally, your rules will be so clear and simple to follow that you will never have to resort to any of the consequences. However, sometimes things just happen.

Remember, all steps on the consequence list come with no yelling, no threats, and no upset. Take deep breaths, get yourself under control, and address the problem simply and quietly. Then continue instruction in as calm and collected a manner as possible. This is not easy! When classroom rules are broken, it is normal to feel angry; but anger serves no useful purpose in resolving the problem and only makes everyone feel more distressed.

Although misbehavior is difficult to face and a challenge to your authority, most of your students will be relieved to know that you care enough about them and their learning to follow through with consequences with as little interruption as possible.

Threats will not work, ignoring blatant misbehavior will not help, and empty promises by students who beg you to not follow the established rules and consequences will never solve management issues. Fairness and consistency will solve the issues.

Maintain a record any time you take action with consequences beyond Step 2 in the consequence guidelines. Repeated misbehavior may indicate significant problems for you and for the student. A modified table such as that shown in Figure 4.3 (see p. 56) provides evidence of the steps you have taken for your own information, for the administration, and for any parent conferences.

Scenario of Possible Consequences

The following is a fictitious case scenario for a classroom disruption involving Bobbie, an 8th grader, in a science class taught by Ms. Menendez. Bobbie is pleasant enough; in fact, she often stops by between classes to just say hello. The problem is that Bobbie is never seated when the bell rings, which is a failure to observe one of the rules. Instead, she is visiting with friends, sharpening her pencil, shuffling through the books on the shelf, or, more typically, chatting with Ms. Menendez at the door.

First sign of a problem—warning. "Bobbie, please sit down and begin the bell work." Of course, this type of warning is given only during the first days of class when Ms. Menendez is making certain that all students understand the expectations for the beginning of class each day. To endlessly repeat a rule means it is ineffective. Pointing to Bobbie's desk and the bell work assignment on the board may be sufficient to get her to work. Ms. Menendez remains calm and in control.

Step 1: Rule is broken—name written on board. "Bobbie, please write your name on the board," Ms. Menendez says, while pointing at the designated area of the board. She continues her instruction as Bobbie writes her name on the board. Because every day starts the same way—with required bell work—Ms.

Menendez does not have to explain anything. Bobbie knows what to do. Alternatively, if it seems easier and less disruptive, Ms. Menendez might simply say, "Bobbie, you are late [not seated, not prepared]; begin your bell work"; and then quietly walk over and add her name to the board. In either case, Ms. Menendez remains calm and in control.

Step 2: Rule is broken again—check mark by name and detention. "Bobbie, I have added a check mark by your name for not being seated when the bell rang and not following directions. Remember that means that you will spend 15 minutes of your lunch break with me. Here is the pass so that you can leave the lunch room and be here by 12:15." Ms. Menendez accepts no excuses and allows no discussion because the rule is enforced by following the steps listed in the consequences. If Bobbie comes in at lunch, the problem should be resolved. If not, Ms. Menendez must locate her, remind her that she is required to come in, and then walk her to the classroom. Waiting to act until later may convince Bobbie that Ms. Menendez is not serious about the rules and consequences.

Another possibility is to have Bobbie stay after class, especially if class is right before recess or lunch or at the end of the day. Even one minute of penalty is highly effective with most students. However, it is important to remain aware that Bobbie has other classes and she does not need to make another teacher upset. If Bobbie rides a bus, Ms. Menendez cannot keep her so long that she misses the bus.

The extra time with Bobbie can be used to further her education, if possible, by giving her a worksheet, a challenge problem, or a similar activity to fill the time and allow Ms. Menendez to attend to her own work. In any case, the number of minutes of penalty time from lunch or recess must be adhered to exactly. If penalty time becomes fun time, Bobbie will not mind breaking the rules because she will get to spend time with Ms. Menendez. Some students will break rules to get the teacher's personal attention.

Step 3: Rule is broken a third time—another check mark and additional detention. "Bobbie, I have had to add another check mark. This means extra time at recess [or lunch]. We have to take care of this problem." Ms. Menendez may be feeling like Bobbie has had too many chances and that this penalty is inadequate. If so, she can choose to not add another check mark and simply move to the next step. Sometimes extra prodding works, and other times it does not. Bobbie may be one of those students who is just acting up so that she can stay in with the teacher, regardless of the consequences. Ms. Menendez may have to reverse her consequences for students who love to stay in: "Bobbie, you may stay in for lunch with me on Friday, but only if you are seated and complete your bell work every day this week."

Some students love to stay in the classroom with the teacher, even if that means extra work. They may be avoiding unruly peers, have problems they need to share, or just want to spend time with the teacher. While fairness must prevail, a new approach may be needed. When Bobbie manages to control her behavior for a day, or other amount of time decided upon by the teacher, a reward such as a lunch with the teacher may be effective. In fact, a reward may well carry over and solve management issues.

Step 4: Rule is broken again—call home. "Bobbie, you have repeatedly refused to be seated and begin your work. The next step is to call your parents so we can remedy the situation." Speaking with Bobbie's parents, Ms. Menendez explains the rule, Bobbie's behavior, the consequence steps taken, and exactly what her expectations are. She wants Bobbie's parents to back her up and help to solve the problem.

Because she is not confident that the phone call has resolved the difficulty, Ms. Menendez decides to ask for a parent conference. Explaining the decision, she says, "Bobbie, you have repeatedly ignored the rule for the start of class. Mrs. Smith, our counselor, has agreed to set up a conference with your parents. I am planning on Wednesday at 3:00. I want you to be there so we can resolve this."

Ms. Menendez knows that repeated offenses are serious. Because neither the counselor nor the principal can attend the conference, she asks her trusted colleague, Mr. Phillips, to join the conference. Before the conference, she asks him to serve as a careful observer but to not say anything during the meeting. She makes clear that she will seek his feedback after the conference.

Step 5: Rule is broken again—outside intervention. Ms. Menendez now faces her last resort. She has talked with Bobbie's parents during a conference, and still the problem has not been resolved. Now it is time to seek outside intervention from disciplinary personnel. She directs Bobbie to go to the assistant principal's office: "Bobbie, please go to the office and see Mr. Sullivan."

Ms. Menendez writes a report for Mr. Sullivan and later meets with him to discuss the situation. He assures her that her sequence of consequences has been appropriate, and his conversation with Bobbie concluded with his sense that she understands the seriousness of her continuing disregard for the rule Ms. Menendez has established. He assures Ms. Menendez that she can count on him for continued support if any new problems arise with Bobbie.

Reviewing the situation, Ms. Menendez knows that the consequence guidelines do not mean that Bobbie will get a warning for each of the classroom rules. Ms. Menendez wants her rules to operate together to maintain control, not to create more problems. If Bobbie is late, has no books, refuses to listen, and disturbs others, Ms. Menendez will address the problem as a whole (lack of courtesy and preparation), not as separate pieces. Bobbie will have moved from breaking one rule to total misbehavior.

Also note that from the beginning of the scenario, Bobbie has been manipulating Ms. Menendez. When she chats with her teacher as the bell rings and nothing is done, she may sense that she can behave as she pleases. Chances are she knows and understands the rule and enjoys getting adults to do what she wants. Immediate and fair enforcement of rules at the outset usually solves issues without further action.

Special Outside Intervention

Some students cannot or will not follow common expectations for classroom behavior. Advice from the counselor, special education teachers, and other staff members who have worked with a particular disability or behavioral issue can help you meet the special needs of those students. Do not act on hearsay about a student's past behavior but, rather, inform yourself with insight from other professionals and your own personal research.

Greg came to my classroom with a terrifying rap sheet. Each of his teachers had been warned of his volatile temper and possible outbursts so we knew to be on guard. One day Greg was having a particularly rough time. He was inattentive and fidgety and not at all focused on our lesson. Suddenly, he jumped up and raced out the door, yelling at other students in the hall. My first impulse was to grab him and yank him back into the room. Fortunately, I quickly realized that this inappropriate, out-of-control behavior would only escalate the situation.

Instead, I pressed the call button for the office to alert an administrator to head my way. I calmly asked Greg to please sit down in the hall and take time to settle down. My evenly composed words affected Greg more than a violent reaction. He complied and composed himself. Although we did not need administrative intervention, I thanked my boss for his quick response and visited with him later to fill in the details of Greg's situation. It was good to know that help was available if I required it; it felt even better to know that I could control my students on my own. Greg later apologized, and we got along well for the rest of the term.

It is never wise to grab a student. Staying calm and in control of the situation may give a student a chance to pleasantly surprise you.

Closing Advice

The ideas you consider as consequences (see Figure 4.2, p. 54) should work in most, if not all, cases. As you determine appropriate consequences, really think about how and why your proposed action will fix any problem.

Repeated misbehavior indicates that something is not right with the rules or the way they are enforced. Examine why a particular rule cannot be consistently followed by a student, and design an action plan together to help students behave appropriately. Many students need one-on-one attention to help them behave, and then they can take personal control. Others require repeated intervention to follow the rules. Although it is usually advantageous to solve all management issues on your own, there are times when you must seek outside help immediately. Again, if a student displays dangerous behavior that affects the student, the rest of the class, or you, do not hesitate to call for assistance.

The majority of students will follow the rules. From kindergartners to high school seniors, students want to learn and they want to please their teachers. Usually it is only a handful of students who disrupt class and then primarily because they need attention or they sense that their teacher is vulnerable. By attending to all problems quickly and fairly, most classroom issues solve themselves.

Nothing in teaching is one-size-fits-all. To keep your rules and consequences effective, you may need to make adjustments during the school year, at a semester break, or for unique classroom situations that arise. Planning and being prepared make a big difference.

5

Meaningful Rewards
and Awards

· · ·

You have diligently determined a set of rules for classroom management and student behavior, thought about how to deal with potential problems in the classroom, defined consequences that match your rules, and outlined the exact steps for consequences to make them work. Now it is time to select methods to reward students for model behavior, dedicated work, and effort.

Rewards are designed to recognize and honor learning and attainment of academic and behavioral expectations. Like everything else in preplanning, they must be carefully considered and wisely bestowed. False or weak praise and accolades along with rewards that have not been fully earned destroy the best of intentions. Rewards and awards pay tribute while promoting growth and learning.

The perfect award or reward for students is as unique as each child. Some children love loud praise, honor, and doodads. Others will withdraw from the scene and then try to never be noticed again when they receive praise in front of their peers. Studying each student and selecting incentives that celebrate and encourage learning enhance the classroom experience. When you focus every tribute on outstanding success, students realize that recognition for their achievement comes through dedication, effort, and educational growth. Plan your awards and rewards by focusing on excellence. Let your students know your learning goals and expectations for them so that success is within reach with diligent, competent work.

The Challenge

My change of heart concerning timed math tests came as I observed a 3rd grade math class. The clock was ticking and pencils were clicking as students recorded their answers. Some problems involved addition; others, subtraction; the majority, multiplication; and a handful of students had moved on to division. All the tests required rapid-fire regurgitation of facts.

"Ding! Ding! Time's up, pencils down. Mark your papers," the teacher cheerfully announced. Students drew a line under the last problem they had solved, counted the total number of problems completed, and then raced to their teacher for their stars for effort and achievement—that is, all of the students except Billy. He continued to work on his math problems as his friends buzzed around him. As the parade of star-seekers ended, Billy quietly grasped his now-finished paper, went to the area where math folders were kept, and slipped the paper into his folder.

I scratched my head and wondered, What is going on? Why hadn't Billy followed the procedures, marked his paper, gotten his star, glowed with pride? Was he cheating so he could get all of the answers done? As the class transitioned into textbook exercises, I sidled quietly over to the math folders and retrieved Billy's work. One glance revealed what Billy had been up to, why he would probably never collect all of his "mad minute" stars or move up to the next level of timed math tests.

Billy was a perfectionist. Every number on his page was written in such exact script that you would think that it had come from a printing press. Slow, methodical precision radiated throughout

Billy's work. Finishing quickly was not a priority for him, but having a flawless, stunning product with correct answers was.

Lessons Learned

What is the goal of having students complete assignments with blinding speed? Are there prizes, awards, and rewards that promote further learning? How (or why) do teachers motivate a student to hurry along when perfection is more significant to the child than speed? Here's a related idea to think about: In the future as you are crossing an expansion bridge, will you hope that the engineers who designed and constructed it considered only how incredibly fast they could get the job done or that it was built with meticulous accuracy over time, with attention to every detail?

There is a reason behind every action and reaction in your classroom. Learning to read these is one key to success.

Rewards and Awards That Honor Learning

So, how will you reward students? There are infinite possibilities, but things that add to and extend learning pay the greatest dividend. The rewards may be as simple as words of positive reinforcement or small tokens such as stickers or school supplies, or they may be as elaborate as a special presentation or a field trip.

Remember, regardless of the chosen reward, it should be linked to educational goals. If you decide to show a movie to reward students at the end of a unit of study, be certain that the movie ties to key concepts that have been the focus of instruction. If you plan to take students to the park, link the walk to an instructional purpose such as gathering leaves for science or generating writing topics for language arts. Many valuable minutes and hours, and sometimes even days, are lost to trivial entertainment. When rewards enhance the learning of students, students profit.

Some rewards are tangible items. They are simple, nice to receive, and support learning. Here are some examples:

- Stickers that recognize excellence, especially those that include descriptive vocabulary
  - Small gifts (badges, cards, games)
  - Pencils, pens, notepads that can also be used in class
  - Nutritious snacks
- Lunch with you—students love this, and it is great for building rapport

As you award the honor to each student, identify why and how it was earned and your expectations for continuing excellence. The right words promote further learning. Students also enjoy rewards such as these:

- Free time for an activity or game that focuses on learning
- A movie based on recent class studies
- Additional time at recess, with the teacher involved
- Games such as Scrabble, UpWords, Battleship, and matching and other card games

Larger rewards may include the following:

- Trade books purchased by you or the school (sometimes available at excellent prices from paperback publishers)
- Field trips to extend understanding of a topic studied. These may be real (which are expensive) or virtual (which can be very inspiring)
- Special projects such as science experiments or cooking experiences
- An award at an assembly for classroom achievement

The key to the selection of honors is being certain that the award is given fairly, that it is significant, and that it promotes further learning for your students. Whole-class awards can be difficult when you have, for example, a student who is frequently absent and never completes his work, making it impossible to close a unit with a celebration of classroom success. You may also have a student who constantly disrupts the learning of peers, making a reward seem inappropriate.

Being fair about rewards is not easy when a few have not earned the honor. It is also unfair to penalize the entire class for the behavior of one or two. Who could imagine that teaching could be so challenging in every way, right down to honoring achievement?

Although any of the suggested rewards works for some students some of the time, what all teachers really want is for students to engage in learning because they love it and want to know more, not because they will get something as a bonus. Individual, specific praise for effort and resulting achievement is a sufficient reward for many students. Any reward must be sincere and represent honor for excellence, which is not the case with trivialities such as rote praise or a galaxy of stars.

When I taught elementary physical education and was assigned to lunch duty, I organized Walk Across America as a lunchtime activity. Each day we covered our mile, and then we indicated our progress on our map of the United States by multiplying the number of walkers by one mile, drawing closer to our destination of Washington, D.C. The walk was open to all students, and each day seemed to draw in more participants.

Students with worries or stresses that they wanted to share managed to position themselves right next to me on the walk so that they could tell me their problems. I listened, and by the end of the mile difficulties often seemed to have been resolved. If concerns continued, the troubled students would be by my side the next day; if matters were easier, they filtered farther back in line where they chatted with friends until they needed me again.

Rewards to students appear in many shapes and forms, but what they most want is care and attention from you.

What conditions and actions deserve rewards? That question is not easy to answer, considering the vast array of students in any classroom. When considering rewards, think about the following:

- What are your expectations for students and their behavior and learning?
  - Do students know and understand your expectations?
  - Are the expectations clear and attainable for all students?
  - Are there exceptions for behavior and learning that need to be considered?
  - Do the rewards build toward better behavior and greater learning, or do they simply represent a momentary honor?
  - Are the rewards academically justifiable?

Realize that even though students may beg for unstructured "free" time as a reward, this option poses many problems that you want to avoid. Even five minutes with no focus can spell disaster.

Celebrating Success

Celebrating student success is fun and exciting. With fairness and consistency in the reward system, all students can be honored. When you love your students and subject area and inject enthusiasm into every instructional moment, students listen, learn, and are motivated to know more. Think back to that teacher who inspired you to learn. It most likely was not fear, intimidation, and disorganization that thrilled you but, rather, enthusiasm, knowledge, and efficient, effective instruction that attracted and sustained your attention and your brain.

When I taught 4th grade, giving Student of the Week honors was simple: 24 students and 24 weeks meant that each student had one week to be honored, with extra weeks available if new students joined my classroom. Because it was expected that every student would be Student of the Week at some point, it was not really an award but something that "happened" to each student.

When I taught junior high, the process was more selective. Out of my nearly 200 students, I was allowed to choose three Student of the Week recipients per year. Thus the number of students dictated that not every student in the school would receive the award. To remedy this perceived systemic problem, I nominated students who had not received many awards and whom I thought would benefit from the recognition. I still carefully weighed student achievement while also trying to boost egos. An odd backlash struck. After receiving the award, my chosen students determined that they were perfect and did not have to do any more work in my classroom.

After several faulty choices, I readjusted my selection process to focus on high achievers who were continuously doing excellent work. On the first round under my new criteria, I pulled my selected student aside and said, "Elisa, I have chosen you as my Student of the Week because of your hard work and dedication in English. You are a wonderful writer and so clever in your thinking. But it seems that every time I give this award, the recipient never does any more work in this class, and I do not want to doom you in this way."

Elisa smiled, nodded knowingly, and then replied, "You do not have to worry about me. I will still work hard for you. But let me warn you about my sister, Rosa. If you give her this award, I can guarantee that she will never work again." A few years later I had Rosa in my class, and I do believe that Elisa had offered me some tremendous insight into her sister!

It is difficult to always be fair in the eyes of every student, but it is important to always try. Sometimes what seems so right is actually very unfair. By paying close attention to your students, studying their work, and reflecting on their classroom achievement, you will be better able to celebrate the individual accomplishments and educational growth of each student.

Closing Advice

It is impossible to stress adequately the significance and responsibility of teaching. An education is based upon instruction and learning, but it extends to so much more. Commitment to excellence rewards you often and in a variety of ways; however, you may never actually see or hear of the results. Students are learning every moment of the day from the way their teachers act, the words spoken, the degree of kindness and caring exemplified, and how effort and achievement are honored and celebrated.

You came into teaching with a deep-seated belief that you can make a difference for children. Your passion and zeal may fade on your roughest days, but remember that they are still there in your heart. Students reflect what their teachers have taught them and the model of living and learning that those teachers emanate.

6

Procedures and Schedules for Flawless Classroom Operation

● ● ●

You have taken critical steps for successful classroom management by establishing a system of clear rules and consequences and planning ways to celebrate the success of every student with rewards and awards that honor student effort and growth while extending learning. Nothing is more indispensible to instructional success than sound classroom management techniques. The next step is to establish in-class and in-school procedures.

Procedures include every type of movement and duty in the classroom. From taking attendance and lunch counts to collecting homework, when teachers have planned and explained their expectations, students know exactly what to do. This effort eliminates needless commotion and confusion, adding minutes to instructional time. An inviting classroom that showcases learning and reflects the personal touches and excellent organization of the teacher is one where students succeed. It also reflects the detailed planning of a clever instructor. Borrowing ideas from your experiences and colleagues can help streamline processes and avoid catastrophes.

The Challenge

During my first year of teaching physical education in high school, I had a student become infuriated with me over jump rope. Rhonda was struggling with a jump rope skill and took her aggression out on me. She flung her rope at me while shouting some vivid obscenities concerning me and the rope. She then began her automatic stomp to the office as I filled out the necessary paperwork describing the incident. She obviously knew she had broken a rule and that the consequence would be a visit to the office. Little did I expect that a "visit" was all it would turn out to be.

After the class resumed and calm slowly returned, I glanced toward the gym door, where I spotted Rhonda as she triumphantly marched into the room and huffed into a corner from which she glared at me for the remainder of the period. After school I consulted my administrator about Rhonda's speedy return to class, stating that I had really needed some time between the incident and Rhonda's reentry into class. He responded, "Get over it." I did, and I also learned to handle most disciplinary action on my own.

Lessons Learned

Sometimes outside intervention solves classroom management issues. At other times it is best to simply solve problems independently. The next time Rhonda prepared to fly into a fury, I was prepared with a procedure (a practice partner) and a carefully delineated description of all the parts of the rope routine to guide her. Future difficulties were averted.

Classroom Procedures and Student Movements

Rules establish expectations for behavior and discipline; consequences reinforce the rules. Procedures cover nearly every other action and student movement within the classroom and the school. When you were student teaching, there were classroom procedures in place that moved instruction along so smoothly that you may not have even noticed they existed. This included actions like handing in papers, getting a drink of water, and going to another class. Clearly defined and practiced procedures ensure that when students have questions, they do not jump up and dash around or wave wildly, disturbing others, but, rather, follow the established guidelines for this procedure. Procedures eliminate confusion, clarify expectations for behavior, and thus maximize learning.

The following procedures are divided into categories that focus on a variety of classroom movements. With practice and enforcement, they solve many potential management issues. Although interruptions such as a broken pencil or drinks of water may not be bothersome in August, by December these additional disruptions can destroy the flow of instruction.

Essential Operations and Basic Equipment

The following suggestions cover most procedures related to everyday operations:

- Sharpening pencils—Allow students to sharpen pencils before class only; if the lead breaks during class, have a can of sharpened pencils ready for a quick exchange.
- Replacing pens that do not work—Have pens ready for exchange.
- Cleaning up after ink and other explosions—Have paper towels and cleaning tools available.
- Retrieving, using, and returning stapler, scissors, and other school supplies—Keep everything stored in clear boxes with attached lids for easy pickup and return.
- Providing extra paper when students run short—Store in an easy-to-retrieve location; especially with secondary students, friends who never have supplies and always borrow from peers can be irritating.

- Providing extra books for students who forget theirs—Are students to be responsible for their books every day, or are you willing to continually provide them?
- Having extra copies of assignments, worksheets, and other activities available for those that have been lost or misplaced—Store in clearly labeled folders placed in marked storage bins.

You cannot plan too much when it comes to having materials available for students.

Collecting Things and Taking Roll

Teachers are always in charge of collecting things. Decide how to efficiently do the following tasks:

- Collecting money for lunch, book orders, fund-raisers—Envelopes with student names alleviate confusion.
- Recording all money collected and storing it in a safe place—Label and lock so no money disappears.
- Taking roll, getting the lunch count, and completing other recording duties—As you take care of these requirements, be certain that students are actively engaged with bell work (see Chapter 9), silent reading, or writing in their journals.

Student Assignments

Teachers are also responsible for the following procedures related to students' work:

- Informing students about missing assignments—Write names of students who are missing assignments on the board; hand each student a note with missing work listed; print a copy of assignments and scores from the grade sheet. Students must know if they have missing work. Tell them what is due and when it is due; then stick to your requirements.
- Allowing students to turn in late assignments or makeup work—Tell students what is due and when it is due; then stick to your procedures for everyone. You will need a procedure for makeup work, but set a firm deadline.

- Having students turn in and hand back papers—Even this procedure must be practiced. By having all papers stacked in the middle of the table or having students in rows hand papers forward from the back to the next student, to the next, and so on, papers are neat, organized, and easy to gather and return.

- Responding to students who are asking questions when you are busy—You must establish boundaries for smooth instruction. Students can write a note to you with their question, ask a designated peer, or use a predetermined signal that they need help immediately.

- Retrieving and returning paper, markers, dry-erase boards, other supplies—Everything comes and goes in clearly marked boxes.

- Cleaning up at the end of the class or the day or after a project—With practice this becomes automatic. Never leave your classroom a mess for someone else to clean up.

Communications

Teachers continually send papers home and await their return. You must manage the following procedures related to communications:

- Handing out required school information forms and then collecting them when signed—As you send papers home, whether in a packet with other work or individually, clearly note when the item is to be returned. Have a folder or manila envelope for each item with a checklist of names attached so you know who still has not returned forms.

- Receiving notes from parents, especially those that require immediate attention—Read carefully and note essential information. Have students deliver these directly to your hand or a specified bin rather than handing them in with other assignments that you will attend to later.

- Interruptions of all sorts, including parents who appear at the door, office requests, intercom interruptions—Keep students busily engaged when you must attend to other business so no minutes of instruction are lost and classroom management is maintained.

Necessities

Various other classroom activities require practice in advance. Think about and plan for the procedures you will use to have students quickly and quietly do the following:

- Get a drink of water.
- Wash their hands for snack, lunch, and after using the restroom.
- Clean up after drinks, snacks, or other spills.
- Go to and from the restroom.

Older students have more self-control and can wait to use the restroom, and they know how to clean up after themselves. With younger students, do not wait. If they need to use the restroom, it is best to let them go immediately. Beware—if one student needs to use the restroom, the rest of the class will have an emergency too. This is true for any age group.

Emergencies

Carefully abide by recommended safety precautions, and follow all designated school and district cleanup procedures. Doing so is critical for the well-being of everyone. Be sure you know the school and district policies for situations including the following:

- Bleeding, vomiting, and other medical emergencies involving students.
- Bleeding, vomiting, and other medical emergencies in which you are the person affected.
- Fire drills, disaster drills, and unexpected crises.

Changing Student Groups

Working in collaborative and cooperative groups, students can learn many things. Of course, this works best when teachers have plans for the following:

- Moving to a partner or a group and back again—This should be done quickly, quietly, without disruption.
- Working in groups and responding to partners—When every student has a role and a responsibility, problems diminish.

Moving to Other School Areas

Students also move about the school and need procedures to make this transition simple. These situations include the following:

- Going to the library or special classes.
- Lining up and preparing for a classroom change.
- Entering and leaving the classroom as a group.
- Going to recess or lunch.
- Remembering to take coats, hats, and gloves to recess in cold weather.
- Retrieving coats, scarves, lunch boxes, and other items left around the school.
- Leaving the classroom to call home or to go to the nurse, the counselor, or elsewhere.

Sometimes it may seem as if students are moving from one place to another far more than they are in class. Smooth transitions and clear expectations for hallway behavior stretch instructional time and ease management problems.

When You Are Absent

When you are absent, extensive planning for the incoming substitute is necessary. If you expect students to behave and learn while you are gone, you must do the following:

- Leave explicit, organized, and detailed lesson plans, including lesson phases, time allotment, student helpers, and other specific information.
- Identify textbooks and other background information to help the substitute locate key materials.
- Clearly identify expected appropriate behavior during your absence.

• Inform the substitute about individual students and their special needs.

• Return to class, understanding that all probably did not go according to plan. Nor will you ever know exactly what did or did not take place in your absence.

Younger students do not know why their teacher is absent and may fear you are not coming back. If possible, let students know in advance of an absence and your expectations for them while you are away. Older students may be set to "sink the sub." By clearly defining expectations before an absence and then dealing with any specific problems upon return, difficulties are alleviated. When students are busily engaged with excellent lessons with the substitute, they find little time for trouble.

Guaranteeing Success with Your Procedures

Even when students know the procedures and have practiced them many times, maybe even for years, they are always ready to challenge them, if allowed. Practice and enforce procedures, and then enjoy the positive results. Remember that when new students come into the classroom, you will need to review and practice procedures with them. These students do not know your expectations for group work or moving to another classroom. Assigning a buddy to help the new student can be beneficial—and it makes the new student feel welcome.

Sometimes little wrenches thrown into the day impede instruction. Perhaps students have entered and are quiet, but have arrived without learning materials (pens, pencils, books, paper). It is often more efficient to lend a pen or offer paper to start the class and then chat with the student about the problem later to find a solution. Another impediment may be a lengthy note from a parent—glance at it to make sure there is no emergency, and place it in a convenient location to read and respond to (if necessary) later so that instruction can flow.

It is wise to pick your battles with care. That is why I suggest giving students supplies until you can determine the problem and work to resolve it without disturbing other students or the lesson. When a student refuses to complete an assignment or to participate in class discussion, search for ways to engage her. Many times what students really crave is attention from the teacher. By building student confidence through thoughtful interaction and encouragement while maintaining high expectations, you are also leading that student to independence. Never complete a student's work for her, but do help her find ways to get the job done.

Weigh each problem independently. If Sue was in a terrible temper yesterday, start today fresh. If Bob never completes his work, yet today it arrives by forklift, reserve judgment (he is finally working/he must have cheated) until you review the work. Recognize that "I don't have my work done" requires a different response than belligerence and hostility. Also remember that blood, vomit, and student safety require immediate attention.

Always be courteous to students. Regardless of how they act or react, remain calm and polite. Often when students (and their parents) strike out at a teacher it is because they do not understand the expectations. Never send students to their lockers, the office, or other places in the school unless there is an obvious crisis at hand and it cannot be solved in any other way. Wandering students create problems.

When I taught 4th grade, as part of the honor of being selected Student of the Week, I allowed the chosen student to help me design the class schedule for that week, excluding pullouts or special classes that could not be tampered with. The student stayed in during the last recess on Friday to create the schedule, which he shared with classmates before they left for the weekend. My students loved this privilege, and I found it refreshing to mix up the order of subjects a little—math first this week, science first the next week, and so on.

For reasons I cannot explain, many of my colleagues hated this approach to scheduling. They said I needed to be more structured and maintain a strict schedule. I bore their criticism and then did what I felt was right. With the added ownership of the schedule, my 4th graders and I accomplished more learning each week. Ownership of learning is a powerful tool; not everyone wants to face creative writing at 8 a.m. and math at 2 p.m. every day. My students looked forward to the variety and loved the sense of being in charge, so the changing format worked well for us.

Daily and Weekly Schedules

Daily and weekly schedules are part of procedures. Some schools have pullouts for all types of reasons and various interruptions throughout the day. A posted schedule is essential for teachers and students.

In most secondary schools that operate on periods, a simple schedule with class times and period numbers suffices. There may be two or three schedules to post, including those for regular class days, block days, or early release/late start days. Any changes—for testing, assemblies, and other reasons—should always be posted in the classroom as far in advance as possible.

Many elementary schools, on the other hand, have a different schedule every day and often special schedules for some students. It is little wonder that teachers and students become confused. Post a daily schedule on large easel paper or on a poster that is clearly visible to all students. Students who go to other classrooms may need individual schedules to keep on their desk or in a notebook. A master copy of the schedule for you, for classroom helpers, or for the substitute serves as a reminder of all of the places students go during the day and week.

Young children just entering school cannot read all of the words on a schedule, so a picture model is appropriate (see Figure 6.1). Determine the important events of the day—entering

Figure 6.1	Using a Picture Schedule

the classroom, story time, play time, math center, lunch time, writing center—and then find pictures or use pictures of students that depict each of the activities. Cut and paste each picture on a note card and put sticky tack or two-sided tape on the back. Post the pictures in the order of the daily schedule near the door or other convenient location that is easy for students to see.

Older students appreciate having a weekly or a monthly calendar that highlights key events, special assignments, and important due dates. Often sales representatives, book publishers, or retail stores in your neighborhood have supplies to share. Post a large calendar with all significant events, such as deadlines for research projects, the swimming or other sports schedule, dates for field trips, end of nine-week periods, picture day, and so forth. As you become more confident in your planning and in determining the amount of time required for each assignment, product, or project, these deadlines can be posted as well. If a date changes, use a sticky note to indicate the new date. (You may need to add a touch of glue to the back of the sticky note to avoid having a student rearrange the dates for you!)

Many students have trained their teachers to repeat again and again. With a calendar in place, all you have to do is point to the area where all answers are provided.

Organization and Storage

Some of the final steps in organizing the perfect classroom setting include the following:

- Organizing bookshelves and storage areas for classroom materials. Label designated areas for
    - Turning in homework.
    - Picking up work that has been corrected.
    - Retrieving makeup work (with clear directions included) after an absence.
    - Turning in notes from home, the doctor, other teachers.
    - Picking up, filling out, and returning late passes.
    - Gathering and returning paper, colored pencils, scissors, and other supplies for classwork.
    - Borrowing books or other needed materials.
- Requisitioning necessary supplies, including pencils, pens, paper, construction paper, rulers, glue, and other items.
- Selecting a chart or list format for checking out books and deciding how to hand out books, record book numbers and condition, and get the books covered and ready for students.

You can use a variety of containers for storage. Here are some possibilities:

- Baskets
- Stack-ups
- Clear storage boxes or bins with attached lids
- Large, clearly labeled envelopes attached to bulletin boards
- Shelves dedicated to specific classroom functions

Clearly designated storage areas save time and eliminate confusion because students know where everything goes and what procedures to follow.

Thoughtful new colleagues may volunteer to help you set up your room. Listen carefully to their ideas, check out their rooms to help develop your plans, and then put your room together so that it works best for you. Sometimes well-meaning coworkers can be overbearing. Be prepared to gather input and then select what fits your style and teaching assignment.

Accept and enjoy assistance, but also be ready to guard your before-school preparation time. If other teachers have classrooms that are ready for the first day of class, they may have free time on their hands while you have considerable planning and setup work to get done. Gently and politely remind them of all you must do and continue your work. Dealing with interruptions is an art you will want to develop.

Bulletin Boards and Classroom Walls

Look around the classroom to determine what to place on the bulletin boards and walls. The classroom should look and feel safe, inviting, and friendly without being too overwhelming. Typically the classrooms that appear overwhelming are elementary classrooms where there are multiple subject areas and a myriad of concepts and posters exhibited everywhere. Some students thrive amid this busy display. Others, however, will be distracted. Secondary classrooms tend to be more austere. Often a picture and a few posters are the only wall adornments. A comfortable learning environment falls somewhere between these two extremes.

Look at your plan for the many months of instruction to determine what goes up first and what can be saved for later. Each bulletin board needs to serve an instructional function. Stuff tacked up here and there with no purpose or meaning does not add to an inspirational learning environment.

To help you decide how to organize information, here are some suggestions for various categories of bulletin board displays:

• Post course, project, and performance expectations, goals, objectives, and desired outcomes based on the current daily and weekly focus of study.

• Display concepts and areas of study to remind students of what they will know and be able to do.

• Exhibit samples of exemplary work. When students can see, study, and think about assignment expectations, they can better understand what their teacher wants and values, and improve their own work.

• Disclose relevant classroom information by posting schedules, homework responsibilities, special messages, and school information.

• Establish an area for late or makeup work, with lesson requirements posted and expectations noted. By making this material easily available, students can collect items independently, without interrupting others.

• Display select posters, pictures, and credentials that tell about you and your educational background, interests, and family. Students are interested in their teacher as a person. When you visit a doctor, don't you check out the diploma and certifications? You should display your own qualifications proudly.

• Create a word wall. Regardless of age group, students need frequent exposure to pertinent vocabulary terms. A display such as that shown in Figure 6.2 saves time with spelling and other questions because students can locate the term on their own. When you teach several subjects and have limited space, you can design a word wall that is used for all subject areas by color-coding the terms. The word wall can grow each day as students work with and study new vocabulary.

• Post announcements. These may be daily announcements for the entire school or special news announcements. Place these where students can refer to them as needed. Do not share any information that is confidential.

Figure 6.2	Math Word Wall

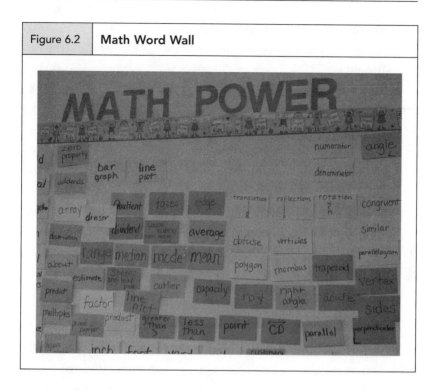

Do not let bulletin boards take over your life. Some teachers spend hours on displays that students barely notice, and the information is never referred to during lessons. Make your bulletin boards a fundamental part of your teaching. Many students will gladly help you design and put up bulletin board displays. Their assistance saves you time and makes them proud that they can help you. As you remove a particularly effective bulletin board display, pack it away in clearly marked envelopes and folders so that you can use it again.

Materials and Supplies

Your school, grade level, subject area(s), and your teaching practices may dictate specific materials for you and your students. The following list, however, is a guide to acquiring basic supplies for your classroom and students:

- Teacher's edition of textbooks
- Adequate number of textbooks for students, plus extras for new students
- Supplementary materials that come with the textbook, such as lesson plans, DVDs, assessments, and other teaching tools
- Paper, both lined and plain, white and colored, small and large sheets
- Pens with blue or black ink
- Pencils, both graphite and colored
- Sticky notes in large and small sizes
- Grading scale
- Grade recording system
- Attendance requirements
- Forms for reporting tardy students
- Emergency codes (fire drill, intruder, medical problems)
- Forms for marking absences and tardy students
- Office, nurse, counselor, special needs referral forms
- Hall passes for students when they leave the classroom
- Rulers, yardsticks, meter sticks
- Plastic containers and zip-seal bags
- Scissors, including left- and right-handed models, and craft scissors
- Tape, including transparent, masking, duct, and double-stick tape
- Paper, including copy, lined, construction, poster, and scratch paper
- Glue or glue sticks
- Note cards
- Paint and brushes
- Cleanup materials, including rags and cleaning solution

Electronic Equipment for Teacher Use

- Computers, printers, ink supplies for teacher and students
- Overhead projector
- Television

- CD or DVD players
- Other electronic devices for classroom use and the supplies that go with each

Daily Student Supplies

- Paper (notebook, graph, computer)
- Pencils, pens
- Pencil sharpener
- Crayons
- Colored pencils
- Markers
- Highlighters
- Sticky notes
- Dry-erase board and marker
- Small storage boxes for materials

Miscellaneous

- Enrichment activities to use when a lesson takes less time than planned or when students need extension materials
- Games for extending learning
- Awards, certificates, and classroom rewards

Most of the items in these lists should be available at your school, but often the supply is limited. A limited supply does not mean that you should hoard but, rather, that you should find out the procedures to be followed for requesting enough to ensure that you have what you need throughout the year.

What you do not have and need, you must buy. It is not uncommon to spend hundreds or even thousands of dollars on students and the classroom each year. Stay alert to bargains, visit the local dollar store or teacher supply store, check with friends and acquaintances who own businesses and have excess supplies they would like to share, go to garage sales, and ask the parent–teacher organization for supplies or funds. Many parents will donate supplies if you ask for items like tissues, extra paper, crayons, computer games, and other goodies.

One purpose of this book is to help you anticipate and solve problems ahead of time to alleviate a bit of stress. At this point, however, you may be feeling completely and entirely overwhelmed, frightened, and plagued with mountains of planning and work to get done. The combination of emotions can be unsettling. Teaching is hard work and requires intensive effort every day. Just remember that getting ready before students arrive on site saves you worry during the year. Each year of teaching does get a little easier, but the job is always enormous. You are in charge of developing the thinking and learning of children—that alone should boggle your mind! Bumps in understanding (class confusion), unexpected surprises (fire drills or unplanned assemblies), and lessons that unfold in less-than-perfect fashion (often sensed as disasters) offer you opportunities to examine your teaching, learn from mix-ups and bewildered students, and thus improve your methods for future instruction. Minor disequilibrium is essential for growth.

Books and More

Students need books and materials for instruction. Handing out books can be simple when teachers are organized. Elementary students can already have their assigned books checked out and placed on or in their desks or storage cubbies. Handing out books to secondary students requires a plan that gets books into their hands with minimal disruption.

One method is to have books already placed on each desk before students enter the room. With a pre-established seating chart (covered later in this chapter), students will know where to sit. After the students are seated, they can write their name in the front of the book, preferably in ink, because it is easy to see and permanent. As students complete forms (such as the Student Interest Inventory in Appendix B) or respond in writing to a posted topic, you can simply walk around the room with a list that includes the name of each student and quickly record the book number and its condition.

Having students call out the numbers of their books can be disruptive; there may be a mix-up in book numbers, which will lead to problems in the spring during book check-in. If your school assesses fines for book damage, you want to be certain of the book's condition at the beginning of the year. With a checklist for things like dog-eared pages or damaged book covers, the end-of-year comparison will be easier and more precise. A parent or volunteer may help with handing out books. Enlisting their help is a good way to get them involved in the classroom from the beginning and allows you to focus on other matters. Be certain that the volunteers clearly understand the expectations for this task—and any time they arrive to help.

If students are required to cover their books, establish this expectation from the outset. Covering books does lessen damage, but it also presents a possible management nightmare. Although half of the students will go home and cover their books perfectly on that first night, others simply cannot or will not complete this task. To remedy this situation, have book covers available in class and then cover the books as a project. If you prefer to have the covering job done at home, be ready for students who have not completed the task. Quick assistance in helping students cover books saves frustration later on. Book covers should not become a discipline issue.

Ron Beck, a government teacher, has made covering books his first assignment to students. After completing an overview of the text and materials to be used during the course, students cover their books with plain paper and then either draw or paste a picture and write information about the Constitution, amendments, presidents, and other relevant topics. Drawings and facts of historical events studied are added throughout the year. The book cover becomes a learning device that is informative and fun. Notice how Ron's assignment solves a problem while also helping students learn.

Regardless of the method of book distribution you select, remember to store the list in a safe place. The list helps trace lost books during the year and makes it easy to collect books from the appropriate student at the end of the school year.

As a getting-to-know-you procedure and to practice correctly pronouncing first and last names, I called roll out loud each period the first week of school. This practice helped me learn student names and correct pronunciation, and it provided an important moment of eye contact to welcome students to class. I had one timid girl, Carrie, who, after I called her name, responded "Here" so softly each day that I could barely hear her. Although she was not so reserved once class discussion began, roll call appeared to be a painful experience.

Because I believe in the power and value of writing, my students always wrote extensively. The more they wrote, the better writers they became and the more their writing became confidential in nature. Later in the year in her writing, Carrie described vivid memories of her childhood. She had hidden underneath the kitchen sink any time her father came home in a rage. As he screamed, he threw dishes, broke chairs, and hit her mother while Carrie trembled, just out of his sight. She then divulged the reason for her quiet response to my calling of her name at the start of the year. Her legal name, the one on all school records, came from a father who had abused her and her mother. Hearing that last name spoken out loud provoked horrible memories. The fact that I did not know about this problem or that the school had no knowledge of these events seems an inadequate excuse for repeatedly re-creating this nightmare for her.

As a teacher, you teach concepts and skills, but the influence you have is far greater than that. Students are very complex, and they need a teacher they can trust.

Seating Charts

One simple way to ease students into the classroom is to have seating charts already complete before their arrival. In elementary classrooms this is most often the norm. However, in some secondary classrooms, the school year begins with students wandering in and taking a seat near chatty friends, with the teacher assigning seats later, thereby losing the opportunity for class to open smoothly. Having preassigned desks and a posted seating chart saves time, confusion, and energy during the first moments with new students.

During that first day and week, assigned seats make many tasks easier, including learning students' names, taking roll, and regulating student movement. A seating chart brings order to the classroom and solves several potential management issues.

There are many ways to arrange the desks or tables to maximize learning and to create easy movement around the room for everyone. Once the class list with student names is in hand, begin arrangement charts with no preconceived notions about students based on gossip and rumor. Listen to coworkers for safety-related issues, but otherwise receive students free of negative background information. How students learn and behave in classrooms reflects their current teacher's caring and organization far more than past incidents with other teachers.

Design your classroom in a way that matches your dream vision for learning. During the first days and weeks of instruction, this dream will transform into reality, and adjustments may be necessary. For example, if the school year begins with students seated in groups of four and you discover that for some talkative students this arrangement is not working, you must review classroom rules and procedures to see if there is something not being enforced to maintain student focus and eliminate side conversations, and rearrange the student seating assignment or desk/table arrangement to maximize learning.

* * * * * * * *

If you quickly move students in a calm, nonchalant fashion, problems are solved with them barely noticing the change. Rearranging seats should not be a topic for discussion or argument, but simply a procedural adjustment.

Here are some suggestions for seating arrangements whether by row or in groups:

- Alphabetical order. This option makes it easier to learn all student names (including correct pronunciation), which should be one of your goals for the first week.
- Male and female students evenly distributed in groups or scattered throughout the room.
- Students grouped by either the same or diverse interests, abilities, or cooperation skills.

Whatever arrangement you choose, keep in mind the following suggestions:

- Seat all students as close to the center of teaching as possible, with an unobstructed view of the teacher. Back row seats or isolated pods detract from focus and learning.
- Avoid allowing students to select their own seats or groups until you are comfortable with their ability to complete assigned tasks with a self-selected group.
- Separate talkative best friends, true loves, and arch-enemies who are unable to focus on instruction; make the rearrangement after students have left the class to avoid disruption.
- Make certain that when working with small groups of students you have a clear view of all students.
- Vary the seating arrangement frequently to increase interaction among students. Keep in mind that some instruction is best delivered to the whole class, whereas other instruction is best when students work with partners or teams.
- Be sure the seating arrangement allows for easy movement and minimal disruption. The real purpose of any seating arrangement is to help students learn and to interact productively with their teacher and peers.

If your teaching assignment requires that groups of students come to your classroom from other classrooms, it is even more important to have assigned seats ready for them. The chances of a quiet, orderly entrance are maximized when seating charts are already established.

Here They Come! Let Them Know Where to Sit

As you greet your students at the door on that first day (and every day until the procedure is understood), let them know what the seating arrangement is. For example, you might say, "Your name is on your assigned seat. Desks are arranged alphabetically by last name." The seating chart can also be displayed on the board or on an overhead with all student names posted. Change the displayed seating chart with each group throughout the day. Another option is to hand students small individual seating charts that help them find the correct seat today and remember the seat tomorrow. You may have to make adjustments during those first days as students move, change classes, or register for school after the first day classes.

Teachers in elementary classrooms often put name tags on each desk. This is a good way for students to find their desks and for young students to have a model of their name to refer to. If there are class changes during the day, use name tags that color coordinate with each group—Group 1 is blue, Group 2 is green—so students can quickly find their seat.

Proximity and Placement

Students' proximity to the teacher and the instruction is important. Even when teachers constantly move around the room, students in the back are often left out. Older students may choose the back of the room to avoid contact and remove themselves from instruction. These students most need their teacher nearby to engage them and prevent behavior problems. The closer teachers are to students, the more attuned the students will be to the lesson and the less chance there is for disengagement or disruption.

Student placement in a classroom has a powerful influence on learning. When I taught junior high and high school French,

I always moved about the room as I was teaching conversation and pronunciation. By listening carefully to my students, I could tell that students in the back of the room had frequently heard my pronunciation differently than those at the front of the room, especially if I had done most of the initial instruction from the front. Proximity and oral repetition helped those students hear the words correctly. Although it may not seem that a few feet would make a difference, it does.

More Name Identifiers

Having name tags for students or other identifiers is absolutely essential in the organized classroom. In elementary classrooms name tags come in many forms and have a variety of uses. They may be tags attached to desks so that students know immediately where to sit. They may be names written on tagboard that is then cut and glued onto clothespins. The clothespins are attached to a ribbon or a strip of paper that is hung by the classroom door. As students enter they retrieve their clothespin and move it to a designated spot to mark attendance and to indicate their choice of hot or cold lunch (or some other information related to a daily procedure). Magnetic strips with names written on them or name tags with Velcro on the back also work well.

Some young students like name badges that they can wear during the day (be aware that little ones may stick themselves when attaching a badge with a pin). The name tags might be attached to string that students can wear as a necklace during the first few days (be aware of the possibility of rope burns). Both of these identifiers are helpful for pullout classes such as art and music where the teacher teaches every student in the school and learning names is difficult. Adhesive labels work well but have limited reuse.

You can also use name tags to be sure that you call on all your students and engage them in learning (see also Chapter 9). Write students' names on Popsicle sticks or tongue depressors, place them in a can or other container, and then draw names randomly to call on students, to assign a job such as handing out papers or taking an envelope to the office, or to divide students into groups. If you have several classes, store each group of sticks in a separate container. As students move, remove sticks for departing students and add sticks for new students.

You can use note cards or index cards in the same way. Have students fill out the cards with name (in large letters), address (for sending notes home), parents' names (to know last names if there have been name changes), phone numbers (for contacting parents), e-mail addresses (for quick contact), and birthdays, special interests, or other information that will help you get to know them individually.

It is a good idea to reshuffle sticks and cards back into the pile after calling on a student to hold the student accountable for the next part of the learning. Sometimes, if you draw a name and then separate it from the stack, the student believes she is no longer responsible for responses, listening, or learning.

It is easy to resort to calling on the same students again and again—the ones waving their hands wildly in the air. But when you do this, many students withdraw from participation. Using the sticks or cards ensures that you keep all students engaged.

At least in part because we could not decide whether to call him Tom, Tommy, Will, Bill, or Willie, our first son has gone by his initials, TW. In the 2nd grade he decided it was time to become more formal. On the first day of school after checking out his name tag, which read "TW," he skipped up to his teacher and announced, "You know, Mrs. Wiggins, I would like to be called Thomas William this year." She nodded and continued class, and when the students headed to recess she began her new work of making a name tag for his desk and several other name displays around the room, each with the complete version of his name.

TW returned from recess and was delighted to see his name magnificently spread across the top of his desk. Other students, excited about his new name tag, began begging for a change in theirs.

Rebecca Christine, Timothy James, Angela Elizabeth, and every other 2nd grader wanted to be called by their full first and middle names. Mrs. Wiggins, the angel that she is, agreed and spent hours creating new name tags for all students who requested it. What's in a name? Quite a bit! What do wonderfully kind teachers do? Please their students.

Closing Advice

Preparing ahead of time by developing procedures, schedules, seating charts, and other elements of an organized classroom makes the beginning of school far easier. Students know teachers care when everything is carefully planned for their arrival. When teachers know their students and build positive relationships, students are quickly drawn into the learning. Children come to school wanting to learn, to understand, and to be successful. When they are engaged from the outset and they know that their teacher cares about them individually, chances for success increase dramatically. All students need a teacher (like you) whose focus is student growth and achievement and who cares deeply about each of them.

Many professions allow employees to put in a day's work and then detach and go home. Teaching is not like that. Teaching draws teachers into the lives and learning of hundreds of students and colleagues. This experience is enriching and rewarding, frustrating and disheartening, and it powerfully develops your strong, compassionate commitment to your profession.

7

Lesson Plans and Unit Plans: The Basis for Instruction

• • •

You have set yourself up for success by learning everything there is to know about school and district policies and where to find correct answers to questions; setting up an organized classroom with every book, paper, and handout ready to go; working out basic rules to create a classroom that is a welcoming and safe place for intellectual development; determining consequences to support the rules; and planning for procedures, schedules, and seating charts that make sense. Now it is time to get to the actual purpose of the job—teaching students.

With the standards and pacing guide in hand (see Chapter 3), you are ready to write lesson plans that will inspire students and generate success. The eight-phase lesson plan template described in this chapter delineates the key components of great lessons, making the best use of every teaching moment. When lessons flow sequentially, always reviewing prior knowledge and then constructing deeper understanding based on new concepts and skills, learning is relevant, organized, and comprehensible. Yesterday's learning is complemented by today's lesson, which leads to achievement tomorrow and beyond.

The Challenge

In college I majored in French and minored in physical education. Why? Because I loved both and knew that each would be fun to teach. I never considered that the two might be a tough combination for someone who might want to hire me. I just wanted to learn more in subjects I loved.

Two French instructors stand out in my mind for deeply expanding my knowledge of the language. Mme. Gambieta was ornery and frightening, and she taught grammar with the power of a hurricane, making clear her extremely high expectations. Each night we had a pile of homework to complete. The next day she would call on one or two of us to go to the board to translate a complicated sentence she had written there. Any mistakes meant a demeaning tirade that each of us dreaded.

Whenever she chose me, I committed errors and then endured her ridicule, which caused me to feel helpless and hopeless as a student of language. No matter how I studied or performed at the board, my work was never of the quality that Mme. Gambieta demanded. I did learn—though through tyranny and fear—and I memorized and eventually mastered her required skills. Fortunately, I loved French so much that she could not defeat me.

The second professor who stands out in my mind is Dr. Bertollo. A tiny man physically, his immense adoration of the language brought magic to everything we did in class, whether it was reading, writing, speaking, discussion, or just taking in his mesmerizing lectures. Each moment in his presence increased my confidence and my love of French.

When Dr. Bertollo described and explained great literary authors and their works, he closed his eyes and transported his learners into an enchanted world of learning. Each class was inspirational and motivational and multiplied my knowledge and understanding. He treated each of us as if we were uniquely bright and gifted. He wanted us to love French language and literature as he did. And we did.

Lessons Learned

These two instructors were each teaching the same subject area to college students, but they possessed very different attitudes about igniting student learning. They were both passionate and knowledgeable, but very dissimilar in their lessons and delivery. I learned, but which teacher and type of lessons best illuminated my learning?

Lesson Plans: Success by Design

It is strange, but some teachers do not complete detailed lesson plans every day and then wonder why students do not learn. Although years of experience can shore up less-than-complete planning, nothing compares to well-planned lessons. Comprehensive plans increase the likelihood that lessons run smoothly, so that students receive quality instruction.

By planning ahead, you are always set for the day. If you become ill, you do not have to drag your sick body from a cozy, warm bed to write plans and then drive in a semiconscious state to the classroom to organize each aspect of the upcoming day, including additional activities and backup materials for a substitute. How nice to remain inert and under the covers knowing that thorough lesson plans are complete and on the desk, with all supplementary material prepared!

Few factors are as vital to teaching success as having well-designed lessons. Imagine a doctor who does not plan adequately for surgery, a contractor who builds a house as he pounds along using scrap lumber and duct tape wherever he finds them, or a teacher teaching a lesson with no foundation or clear direction. Students attain desired learning outcomes through excellent lessons. Creating the plans should not take longer than presenting the actual lesson—but it may feel that way at first.

Textbooks and supplementary materials for the subject or grade level provide many lesson plan outlines, strategies, and activities. Being fully familiar with the materials and with grade-level and subject requirements leads to solid instruction. Excellent materials sit on shelves or are available online while teachers spend hours trying to design lessons instead of taking advantage of what already exists. Refer to and implement ideas and lessons from these materials, and then modify or fill in when no available tool can adequately meet instructional needs.

Lesson Plan Phases

After studying, observing, and reflecting upon lessons and lesson plans for many years, I have manipulated and adapted ideas to create a sequential design that reaches each diverse learner. Although on-the-spot modifications are almost always necessary while teaching, I use an eight-step model that engages students by building on their knowledge. The design provides many opportunities for teachers to recognize and correct students' misconceptions while extending understanding for future lessons.

Phase 1: Introduction

- **Set a purpose.** Describe the overarching reason for this lesson.
- **Introduce the key concepts, topic, main idea.** Get students on the right track. This step may be a note on the board, a diagram, or a probing question of the day's lesson focus.
- **Pull students into the excitement of learning.** Seize students' attention with items like an amazing fact, a funny quirk, a challenge, or other mind tickler.
- **Make the learning relevant.** Explain how this lesson extends past learning and leads to future learning—that is, the significance of the concepts, skills, and focus of the lesson.

Phase 2: Foundation

- **Check on previous knowledge.** Verify what students already know.

- **Clarify key points.** Double-check on learning from the past.
- **Focus on specific standards, objectives, goals.** Link the lesson to the standards, and let students know exactly what they will know and be able to do as a result of this lesson.
- **Check for correctness and add to background knowledge.** Add extra information for the day's learning and beyond—just enough to launch into the main lesson.
- **Introduce key vocabulary.** See it; say it; read it; write it.

Phase 3: Brain Activation

- **Ask questions to clarify ideas and to add knowledge.** Engage students in the learning and build background with probing questions.
- **Brainstorm main ideas.** Fill students' heads with ideas, concepts, possibilities; allow them to expand and clarify their thinking.
- **Clarify and correct misconceptions.** Engage students in activities that will inform you as to whether students are confused or have incorrect ideas so corrections can be made before the misconceptions become worse or detrimental to learning.

Phase 4: Body of New Information

- **Provide teacher input.** Lecture, add key points and new information, read the text or articles, and solve problems. Present the body of the lesson. This may be a whole-class lecture, a small-group activity with teacher supervision, or a partner activity with teacher supervision. The learning is active (not silent reading without specific goals or mindless completion of a worksheet).

Phase 5: Clarification

- **Check for understanding with sample problems, situations, questions.** Have students practice with the information just taught. Guide the learning.

Phase 6: Practice and Review

- **Provide time for practice and review.** Allow students time to practice under your supervision. You and the students work together.

Phase 7: Independent Practice

- **Supervise students' independent practice.** Select additional strategies for small groups of students who still do not "get it." Other students may begin to work independently, with the final goal being that all students can work on their own. This practice prepares students for successful homework, and it prepares them for future learning.

Phase 8: Closure

- **Bring the lesson to closure.** Link the lesson phases and information together. Summarize the learning of the day, and discuss how it fits into the big vision for learning. Have students demonstrate what they know and can do by writing a brief note to hand in as they leave; the note may include questions, problems, or ideas on the learning. Alternatively, they may write in their journals or explain their understanding to a partner.

Lesson Plan Template

Figure 7.1 shows a sample lesson plan for an 8th grade history lesson on the Civil War. The key parts of the template underlying the lesson plan are the following:

- Time allotment—How much time to spend with each lesson phase, such as the introduction and the body of new information.
- Lesson phase—An explanation of the elements of each phase.
- Details—Space for writing a supply list, page numbers, predetermined discussion questions, and other key lesson points.

Figure 7.1	Sample Lesson Plan

8th Grade History Lesson on Civil War		
Time Allotment (Minutes)	Lesson Phase	Details
5	**Introduction** Set a purpose. Introduce the topic with a grabber and information to get students thinking. Make the learning relevant.	Write the phrase "All men are created equal" from the Gettysburg Address. Have students explain what this phrase possibly meant in the 1860s.
5–10	**Foundation** Check on previous learning. Clarify key points of the coming lesson, including standards, goals, and objectives, building background knowledge and key vocabulary.	Quick discussion of the grabber. Discuss slaves, women, uneducated white men, educated white men. Goal: To explain the significance of the Gettysburg Address in American history and to link the learning to voting rights today. Key terms: *equal, conceived in liberty, dedicated, proposition*
5	**Brain Activation** Ask questions; clarify; provide additional background knowledge. Perhaps include a brainstorm activity on the topic to check learning.	What do the words mean? Why did Lincoln phrase his speech this way? What would happen today if Lincoln gave this same speech? What do we know about the United States in the 1860s based on this speech? How does the phrase "All men are created equal" tie to the rest of the speech? To history at the time? To a deep understanding of American history? How does the opening paragraph lead to the ideas of paragraph two? Paragraph three?

(continued)

Figure 7.1	Continued

8th Grade History Lesson on Civil War		
Time Allotment (Minutes)	**Lesson Phase**	**Details**
10–15	**Body of New Information** Build background knowledge, lecture, and introduce key new points of understanding, correcting misconceptions. Read text; complete whole-class problems; conduct class discussion.	Discuss the Battle of Gettysburg; refer to information on pages 273–281 in the textbook. Discuss pictures of battle on pages 282–285. Write key notes/ideas on overhead. Have students add information to history notes.
5–10	**Clarification** Provide sample problems and situations. Pose questions to move students toward independent work.	Students write their reflections on the information presented in the text in their notebooks/journals.
5–10	**Practice and Review** Students work with teacher and whole class, in small groups, or with a partner to clarify learning.	Discuss in small groups the significance of the speech, the battle, the fact that President Lincoln came to the battlefield to make the speech, the turning point of the Civil War.
10	**Independent Practice** Students practice on their own. Begin homework. Struggling students get additional practice.	Students select two or three other key phrases from the Gettysburg Address and write a brief summary of each.
5	**Closure** Connect the lesson details together. Answer questions and respond to whole-class difficulties.	Students share phrases with a partner. They write their favorite phrase with a brief explanation as to why on an "exit pass." Teacher collects exit passes as students leave to assess learning and understanding and to use as a guide to tomorrow's instruction.

The plan assumes a time slot of 50 to 70 minutes. Because a period or day has a finite number of minutes, it is critical to plan lesson phases carefully. (See Appendix A for a template you can use to plan a 50- to 70-minute lesson.)

As the lesson is taught, the teacher pays close attention to how well students understand key concepts so she can later write notes in her lesson plan book to inform future lessons. Every detail, from the minutes necessary for each phase to notes concerning the best questions for student response, provides insight for the next lesson.

Pacing the lesson means balancing content delivery, practice time, and checks for student understanding. If the opening of the lesson lasts 15 minutes, less time is available for the main focus and practice that are necessary to improve skills. A brief introduction that draws students into the learning transitions them into the heart of the lesson with adequate time left for questions and practice. The same is true if the main portion of the lesson lasts for 45 minutes of a 50-minute period. Students will not have time to review and apply their learning or practice independently before they leave the classroom with homework that they may not understand. Because teachers expect homework to be done completely and correctly, they must be certain that students have the skills to accomplish the task.

A timer can help you practice pacing lessons. A kitchen timer with a short beep when time is up does not disturb the class and reminds you of the time elapsed. A timer on the overhead or projector screen is also useful for keeping students on task because they can see the seconds ticking away as they work. When students know they have a set number of minutes (always slightly less than it seems it will take them to complete the task), they stay on task and finish within the time slot. Good timing means all lesson phases can be completed.

When I work with teachers, it scares me to death when they inform me that they do not have a lesson plan or do not have anything special planned for the day. Every day is special, every day students need to learn, and every day you must have a plan. Change your plan, modify it, carry parts over from today's to tomorrow's lesson, but never, ever leave school without lesson plans for tomorrow and the upcoming week.

Essentials to Learning: Practice and Closure

Most teachers have lessons that contain an introduction and a body or main focus (Phases 1 through 4), but several of the other phases are missing. It is crucial that students receive adequate information and are able to understand and apply it accurately when they are on their own. This is why Phases 5 through 7 are so important. You can think of these phases in these terms:

- "I do"—Clarification (Phase 5: Teacher demonstrates, explains, models for students)
- "We do, we do, we do"—Practice and review (Phase 6: Students and teacher work together)
- "You do"—Independent practice (Phase 7: Students work independently)

By incorporating these phases into lessons, you ensure that students understand the lesson (because they have observed your demonstration or heard your explanation) and that they can continue working outside class (because they have practiced and have models to refer to).

An excellent closure activity is the exit pass (Figure 7.2, p. 113). On a note card or small piece of paper, students respond to a question you have posed orally, summarize what they have learned in class, or ask their own question about the learning or lesson. Student responses in these sorts of closure activities provide you with instant feedback for adjustment of your instruction. If another group of students is coming to class for the same lesson, you can make modifications based on the information just gathered from your students. This feedback is also helpful for determining the effectiveness of instruction.

Figure 7.2	Sample Exit Pass
Student's name: Summary or your response to learning/lesson: Question about today's learning:	

Char Owen, a 4th grade teacher with many years of experience, calls her exit passes "passports." She uses them as a ticket to recess or lunch. The passes transform into "passports" with several pages, and the students' responses become their visas and stamps from countries (learning) they have visited. After each of Char's lessons, she writes her lesson reflections on a manila folder designed around the key concepts of the unit of study. She indicates what went well and what needs reteaching and creates a table of contents for the papers inside the folder. The handouts and activities in the folder are readily available if she needs extra copies now, and everything is ready for future lessons as well. She simply pulls out the folder, gathers materials she needs and copies them, places a check mark on the front to show what she has used, and then returns the masters to the folder.

Lesson plans are essential for clear, organized instruction. Although they are time-consuming and sometimes tedious to prepare, never be caught without them. When planning is incomplete, timing and organization are off and students suffer.

Additional Considerations for Planning Great Lessons

As you plan your lessons, keep the following things in mind:

- Attention span of your students, age group, and diversity of learners.

- Complexity of material and time requirements for each instructional component.
- Decisions concerning whether whole-class presentation, small groups, or partners are best for teaching and learning a particular concept.
- The best configuration of student groups for optimal learning, for example, homogeneous or heterogeneous ability groups, complementary interests, or personalities that work well together.
- Activities that best facilitate the learning of each student.
- Preassessment of skills and background knowledge to determine what students already know, what they need to know, and what their misconceptions are.
- Selection of regular and supplemental materials to augment learning.
- Strategies for frequently monitoring and adjusting the lesson.

As you think about lesson plans, consider the following:

- Is there enough information written to make the lesson clear?
- Have you selected a variety of activities? Are the goals and objectives clear and attainable, and do they match the proposed instruction?
- Does this lesson build on previous knowledge and lend itself to future lessons?
- At lesson's end, are students set for independent success?

Good lesson plans are always well worth the effort. During my first years of teaching I always had the plan book opened on my podium for easy reference as I walked by during instruction. Later, after writing the formal plans I created note cards with reminders to carry with me so that I did not have to refer to the formal plans as often.

For my junior high and high school students, I designed a study guide. The guide highlighted the goals, objectives, assignments, and due dates for one or two weeks at a time so students knew what we would be learning. Every step I took in planning led to ease of implementation. Even plans I had to discard because they ended up not meeting the learning needs of my students increased my knowledge and understanding of the essentials of good lessons.

After the Lesson

After each lesson, consider what went well and what needs to be adjusted. This is easily done with a postlesson appraisal, such as the one in Figure 7.3. Great teachers always reflect on their lessons. An appraisal form can also be completed by paraprofessionals, volunteers, or substitute teachers who have worked with your students to provide feedback on their instruction and student learning.

In addition to critiquing your own lessons and lesson plans, ask students to give you feedback on the lesson quality, organization, clarity, and goals reached. This feedback is especially beneficial when students analyze a unit of study that may have caused them to struggle with time management, such as a unit involving a research paper. A question I use is "What will you do differently next time?" The best-ever answer: "I'll have my mom get started a lot sooner so next time she can do a better job." Sometimes lesson feedback is more insightful than you could ever imagine.

Figure 7.3	Postlesson Appraisal

1. What went well? Why?

2. What needs work? What will I do to improve the lesson?

3. What do I need to do in tomorrow's lesson? How will I get it done?

4. What special considerations are there, and how should I handle them?

5. Additional comments and thoughts:

Students Who Miss Instruction

When students are in class as the lesson is presented, you can observe and get feedback from them concerning what they know and what needs repeating. Some of this is obvious in the work they complete; other indicators come from the expressions on their faces and the questions they ask. When students have been absent or they have late work and missing assignments, lessons often require adjustment. Late work and makeup work affect today's lesson plan—and tomorrow's. As work is collected, remember that students returning from an absence may have gaps in learning that need to be filled in.

Late work presents its own special problems. There are several factors to consider:

- How late is late?
- Why is the work late?
- Is turning in work late a pattern or a rare event for this student?
- What were the goals for the assignment? Was one goal that students complete their work to determine proficiency?
- Was there another reason for the assignment?
- What are the desired outcomes of the learning?
- Is the assignment designed for learning, practice, and to cement understanding?
- What is the expectation for the work beyond a grade in the grade book?
- If students rarely do their homework on time and then want to slide it in as late work, what is the policy?
- Is it more important to do the work as required (even if not doing the homework does not hinder learning) or to understand the material?
- Will the student be able to succeed in this grade or subject without completing this assignment?

For every rule on homework and late work, you will likely find a viable reason for some students to break the rule. Clear policies are important, but so is flexibility. Sometimes things happen to the most diligent students. Make sure that you know the school's policy—or that you develop your own policy—for the following:

- Late work
- Makeup work
- Extenuating circumstances
- Incomplete work
- Unidentified work

No matter how well-planned lessons are, there are always things that just happen. Time and practice make lessons flow more smoothly. The more you teach, the more experience you gain and the greater the number of activities and strategies you will have in your repertoire for excellent instruction.

I spent my 4th grade year in a combined 3rd/4th grade classroom of 33 students. Kind and wise Mrs. deCoursey was my teacher, and I loved her. One of our topics in social studies was learning about all 50 states. We drew maps and studied information about each state, such as the capital, state bird and motto, main industries, and geographical features. Mrs. deCoursey made every lesson wonderful and fascinating, and I can remember her instruction more than 45 years later.

As we neared the end of the unit on the United States, we divided into groups of three or four. Each group received a large piece of plywood on which to create a replica of the assigned state from a mixture of flour, salt, and water. After working for days to get every mountain, river, valley, and lake exactly in place, we painted our model, labeled key cities, and placed pennants across the state to mark natural resources and industries.

Each group shared its findings by presenting our culminating projects to the applause of our classmates. It was a learning experience that I will remember forever. It was fun, well organized, engaging, purposeful, and educationally sound, with clear learning goals—everything a unit of study should be. This unit of integrated study included social studies (the states), geography (location and physical features), language arts (research), art (the map), mathematics (dimensions), and economics (industry) combined into a multiweek time period.

Review of Lesson Planning

Carefully designed lesson plans are essential to clear, organized, and engaging lessons. They include the following elements:

- A link to past learning that draws students into new learning
- All eight lesson phases, including time for practice with the teacher, with peers, and independently
- Ongoing checks for understanding
- Adjustments to meet the needs of diverse learners
- Closure that ties all lesson phases together
- Timing that maintains interest and engagement throughout the lesson

Lesson plans are not little snippets here and there to get you through the day. They are linked day to day, week to week, throughout the year. You do not teach multiplication today and then set it aside, never to be reviewed or practiced again. Teaching and lesson plans are not check-off lists but a continuing process that when placed together create a larger product—a unit of integrated study.

Unit Plans: Daily Plans Linked by Concepts

Unit plans consist of concepts and learning goals that are taught over a period of time and are woven together, often across subject areas. A unit plan lasts two or three weeks (or longer) and includes several standards, skills, and desired outcomes for interconnected learning. For example, science research involves the research, reading, and writing strands of English/language arts. So while the students are studying, researching, and writing about amphibians, they are using the skills they have learned and practiced in language arts as they expand their knowledge about science concepts. Combining subject areas most often involves overlapping lessons in the subjects, thus creating longer spans of class time for study and practice.

At the secondary level, unit plans contribute to optimal learning when teachers of different subjects work together to develop cross-curricular studies. When unit plans are done well, learning is maximized through multiple exposures to key learning concepts and goals. For example, with the topic of modern art, students study and replicate particular art pieces in art class, read about great artists in English class, and compare the history of art and historical events affecting art in social studies.

As a beginning teacher, do not think that you must spend hours and hours planning so that all lessons fall underneath the umbrella of a unit plan. Begin by knowing that each lesson is linked to the next and then to ensuing lessons. Common concepts, recurring themes, and similar desired outcomes, along with instructional materials that blend diverse subject areas, plus a big vision of student learning, overlap to create a unit plan. Many of your teaching colleagues are likely to have unit plans they have already developed and used and are willing to share. Take advantage of this free material and then adjust it for successful implementation with your students.

Elements of a Unit Plan

A unit plan overarches all daily lesson plans with connections among key topics, concepts, skills, and desired outcomes. All the following elements should be considered when developing a unit plan:

- A principal purpose
- Main topic or topics (e.g., World War II, reptiles, double-digit multiplication)
- Concepts (e.g., integrity, the Doppler effect) that unite lessons within the unit
- Essential skills to be developed

- Academic goals and desired outcomes
- Academic standards that directly relate to the subject area or areas
- Cross-curricular connections
- Methods to make the learning relevant throughout the unit
- Big ideas that link to additional big ideas to increase understanding
- Past learning that links to present learning and leads to future learning
- An understanding of students' current knowledge
- Questions to guide thinking each day and from day to day
- Questions based on recurring unit ideas or themes
- Clear expectations for learning of all students
- Vocabulary to study and focus on, with multiple exposures over time to engrain learning
- A determination of appropriate level of proficiency to meet desired outcomes
- Assessments for before, during, and after lessons and the overall unit

Begin with an Outline

To begin planning a unit, first outline the academic goals of the big vision of the unit. This phase includes deciding what students should know and be able to do at the end of the unit, the number of days or weeks required to maximize learning (great units always require slightly more time than expected), and selecting textbook chapters and stories and other materials to incorporate.

Next divide everything into the available class periods or time slots to determine how to fit the pieces into the unit. Build in extra time for review and enrichment to ensure that all students have learned the material. With each lesson, pinpoint the specific goals and desired outcomes that are to be met to ensure your students will meet the learning goals of the overall unit. Document shortcomings and successes for future lessons.

When you know where you are going, you have a far better chance of arriving at your destination. Planning your unit road map for learning is an excellent way to stretch your thinking and implement the big vision. Having a clear goal and deciding what routes best allow you to reach your destination increase the likelihood of success. The stops along the way for refueling and refreshing are the strategies and assessments that enhance the trip and the total learning experience.

Overarching Questions for Unit Planning

As you plan each unit, ask these overarching questions:

- What is the big vision for the unit?
- What is the primary educational intent for this unit?
- What do students know right now?
- What should students know and be able to do by the end of each lesson?
- What should students know and be able to do by the end of the unit?
- How can instruction be adjusted to meet the needs of all students?
- What will take place before and during the unit to make sure that all students are successful?
- What assessments (see Chapter 10) will best ensure that all students have reached the desired outcomes? These should include the following:
    - Pre-assessments
    - Mini-assessments
    - Post-assessments
    - Monitoring and adjusting throughout the unit
- What happens when students do not know?
- What materials are available for enrichment activities?
- What are the cross-curricular connections?
- Is the time for the unit well justified?

The purpose of a unit is to unite lesson plans to enhance learning. The unit plan is not a place to throw together every imaginable teaching idea in total disarray. I have witnessed magnificent castles created from units that had nothing to do with academic standards or what students needed to know and be able to do. The students had fun as they built models and colored pictures, but the deep learning was not present. On the other hand, units that are artfully crafted provide tremendous learning opportunities for students.

Unit plans demand great amounts of time, energy, and planning, but the results are incredible because each step of the learning ties to the next. The planning outline in Figure 7.4 is useful for completing the specifics of a unit.

Unit Plans, Time Slots, and Grading Periods

An important factor to consider in planning is where lessons and units fall in the grading period. Sometimes long units create problems when the "big grade" lands in the next grading period. If the culminating project is due at the beginning of the new nine-week period and it has a weighted grade, that one big grade might distort the true picture of student learning. A high mark may indicate to some students that the rest of the learning for the new nine-week period is of no significance—the kind of attitude expressed by comments such as "I already have an *A*." A low mark may be followed by "I didn't finish my project, so it is useless to try to improve my grade." Plan the unit with these excuses in mind to alleviate potential problems.

Unit Essentials and Considerations

As you plan and teach the unit, constantly ask, "Can I prove that students have learned? What will I do for those who know and those who do not know?" These questions and reflective responses ensure that all students will understand and achieve. If done well, unit plans combine lessons in a way that can lead to extraordinary student knowledge and understanding. It is an inspirational sight when students light up with "aha!" moments through multiple encounters and practice with concepts and skills that infuse their learning.

Figure 7.4	Unit Outline
Purpose of the unit:	
Unit title:	
Key concepts:	
Subject area(s):	
Desired outcomes:	
Overarching goals, big ideas:	
Overarching standards to be studied:	
Sectional standards:	
Daily standards:	
Daily big ideas:	
Sectional goals:	
Daily goals:	
Overarching questions (that reflect and highlight the big ideas):	
Sectional questions:	
Daily questions:	
Assessment types to be used: Informal: Formal:	
Methods to monitor and adjust instruction during lesson:	

(continued)

Figure 7.4	Continued
Methods to determine background knowledge:	
Key vocabulary: Tier 1: Necessary for student success; students should already know or be familiar with these; fairly easy to teach Tier 2: Necessary for student success; primarily new terms or the development of deeper understanding of the terms Tier 3: Difficult, problematic terms; specific to domain	
Materials needed:	
Time allotment per day:	
Number of days required to complete the unit:	
Desired outcomes based on previous lessons and student progress:	

Daily plan for lesson phases (include as many days as necessary):
 	
    Day 1:
 	
    Day 2:
 	
    Day 3:	

Methods for connecting all learning:	
Next steps:	

Cross-curricular unit plans offer the opportunity to work with respected colleagues to increase insight, add new perspective, and augment instructional knowledge. This teamwork expands your own expertise while also demonstrating your special skills to others. However, not all colleagues will exert the same effort for each unit. Avoid making big unit plans with those who do not willingly complete their part of the planning and instruction or who do not appreciate your enthusiasm.

When I was teaching 8th grade English, we read *Night*, the autobiography of Elie Wiesel. The book details the author's survival in a concentration camp during the Nazi terror of World War II. I taught this unit for 11 years, and each repetition and reading made the book more powerful to me as lessons were enriched through student feedback. I scheduled the unit during the time that my students were studying World War II in history class, creating a learning liaison between the two subjects.

Each year my students talked more and more about the unit, comparing facts and information from their history teacher and textbook to what we were learning from the autobiography and our discussions. The effect of this unit expanded greatly when the history teacher, Herk Criswell, and I began more detailed planning of our units together. The students did not just double their knowledge between our two classes, lectures, notes, and discussions. I would say they tripled or quadrupled their knowledge. It was amazing to see the enthusiasm they gained for learning through our collaboration.

A bonus was how students compared the historical information each teacher shared. As we would read and discuss, some would say, "Yeah, that is exactly what Mr. Criswell said in history." On other occasions, students would double-check our facts: "Mr. Criswell told us.... But you said...." This interchange led to interesting dialogue about perceptions of what students had heard in one class or the other and how history is interpreted by readers, writers, textbook companies, teachers, and students. It also allowed students to compare the style and tone of two literary genres: autobiography and textbook.

Sometimes my students would comment, "Hey, did you know we are learning about this in history?" and I would nod, to which they would respond, "Why don't more teachers do that? It really makes things make sense when you hear about them more than once." Although the unit was always complicated and demanding to teach, the student learning and thinking were extraordinary and empowered both teachers and students.

Being Aware of What Students Already Know

Whether you are working on daily plans or a large unit, always consider your learners. Understanding their background knowledge and previous learning prevents needless repetition or insufficient explanation. Students bring a wide variety of background knowledge with them to every class and subject, and part of teaching is determining the extent of that knowledge.

Experience with students shows that one of the best frames for initial instruction in a unit is the KWL (Ogle, 1989), which asks the following: What do students (1) know, (2) want to know, and (3) learn as a result of the unit? At the beginning of the unit, students complete the *Know* section of the KWL. The teacher now has background knowledge about past learning and can also identify any misconceptions. Next the students complete the *Want to know* section so that the teacher can interweave bits of information that have piqued curiosity into the contents of the unit. At the end, students complete the *Learned* section to provide feedback about their understanding, which the teacher can then use for planning next steps.

Every step you take to set students up for success in learning pays high dividends. One of these is the bright smiles of achievement on student faces as they "get it." Another is the deep personal satisfaction gleaned from doing a job well. Few rewards are greater than positively affecting the lives and learning of children.

Closing Advice

Teaching is a conglomeration of best teaching practices, intricate lesson and unit plans, and the expertise of the teacher guiding students to learning. It is exhausting and exhilarating. Those who remain in the profession over time develop a tremendous knowledge and understanding of children, their perceptions, and how young minds work. Although you may not make the multimillion-dollar salary of a sports celebrity, a movie star, or a CEO, your reward for teaching will be worth far more.

On the most troubling days, when frustration and worry levels appear to be at their highest, remember that there is nothing more exciting than observing students when the "Aha! I get it" light pops on. You may never know the difference you made in the lives of students, but teachers always leave a mark. Great lessons and well-planned units increase knowledge and leave imprints of competence and understanding.

Teaching and learning are a never-ending cycle. Although all of the work may wear you out, when students' minds shine, you will be refreshed and ready for the next challenge.

8

Time
Management

• • •

You have created detailed, eight-phase lesson plans and considered ways to incorporate lessons into unit plans. Now you can focus on ensuring the value of your instructional time.

Virtually everyone wishes for more minutes in the day. Although you cannot manufacture minutes, you can make certain that your teaching time is filled with high-quality instruction and engaged student learning. Excellent lesson plans presented with smooth pacing lead students step-by-step through learning. Clocks, timers, and careful preparation ensure impeccable timing as teachers move effortlessly through key lesson components. Surprise! Practice and preparation produce wise time management!

The Challenge

One of the most demanding classes I ever taught was secondary remedial reading. One year the class was made up of 25 boys, most of whom were focused on disruption rather than learning, and one shy little girl. My lessons and teaching style were extremely structured, and I barely allowed time for catching an extra breath to prevent these students from demolishing any chances for teaching and learning. Although I frequently tried to engage and reengage the group in class discussion about our reading and writing, we seemed to always have to revert back to silent reading and worksheets to maintain classroom control.

Fellow teachers could not understand why I had to be so strict until we exchanged teaching assignments for a day. As my colleagues tried their best teaching and engagement strategies—techniques that worked flawlessly with other students—my students could not settle down and behave or listen to what any of them had to offer.

I had several substitute teachers during the first semester, each of whom refused to come back after spending a class period with this group of loud, rude, and obnoxious students. I was pretty frustrated myself, but I never completely abandoned hope that somehow I could reach them.

With unending perseverance on my part, their behavior and attitude slowly began to improve a tiny bit as they realized the benefits of learning. By the beginning of the second semester, I could relax occasionally, and we held short discussions about our reading. Their knowledge and reading ability began to grow. By May, I finally knew I would survive and so would they. The most convincing evidence of this came one hot, sultry afternoon. I was almost eight months pregnant, exhausted, and the heat was about to put me away. We were seated in a huge round-table configuration, reading and discussing key points. I was so tired. I stretched, I wiggled, I yawned, I fought drowsiness, but finally I gave in. I dozed off. It was when my book toppled out of my hand and clunked to the floor that I was startled awake. The kids laughed and said, "Welcome back," and then continued their group work.

Lessons Learned

When teachers manage time and carefully structure each instructional minute, a mutual respect slowly develops with students. It may require much patience and huge reserves of energy from the teacher, but once students finally accept that their teacher will not give up on them, they can apply their talents toward learning.

Balancing Time and Instruction

Time management is easier when you have deep content knowledge of your subject area and recognize the learning needs of students. Teaching entails selecting from a multitude of varying strategies and activities for the ever-changing conditions in the classroom. Regardless of how detailed and organized the lesson or how careful your demonstrations and explanations, surprises and questions always arise. It is essential to respond to these while still maintaining pacing and timing to complete the lesson.

Well-Designed Plans

Planning well-designed, comprehensive lessons and units assists in achieving the following:

• Creating the big vision of learning and the desired outcomes for the learning.

• Clarifying assignments and expectations for yourself and your students.

• Preparing backup activities for students who complete work quickly or for those who need additional practice.

• Organizing extra materials for whenever there are leftover minutes of class time.

• Ensuring that all students are engaged and learning throughout the lesson.

• Making certain that every student succeeds.

• Building knowledge about what will work or will not work in future lessons.

Beginning teachers generally have one of two problems. Either they have more than enough materials organized to fill the class period and find that they rarely get through their lesson plans, so gaps develop; or their lessons speed by with inadequate discussion and practice, concluding with empty time and no additional activities planned. Matching instructional minutes to desired learning is a skill that improves through experience and awareness of time.

Well-paced and stimulating lessons engage students in instruction, practice, thinking, and active participation. Disengaged students are more likely to be distracted and disruptive and to create classroom management nightmares. Focused, concise lessons with specific learning goals coupled with precise pacing increase productivity and solve most classroom management issues, leaving more time for teaching and learning.

Getting Time on Your Side

How do good lesson plans, time management, and classroom management fit together? Lesson plans that manage each minute of classroom instruction with no lapses increase the likelihood that students will be engrossed in learning and goals can be attained.

The perfect lesson plan for tomorrow begins at the end of school today. Every afternoon before you leave school it is essential to do the following:

• Review today's lesson plans and add notes about the successes and stresses of the day.

• Reread and rework tomorrow's lesson plans as a continuation of today.

• Lay out or stack up all of the materials and supplies needed for instruction tomorrow, including

    - Book opened to the correct page and special supplies organized,

    - Bell work (see Chapter 9) or other class starter posted on the board,

- Handouts and activities placed in the order of intended use, and
- Checklist of to-do items such as collecting makeup work from students who were absent or noting students who need additional instruction.

The best teachers are meticulously well prepared. They want everything to run perfectly so that classroom minutes maximize instruction and learning. Teachers who are in control always appear calm, while their frazzled colleagues track down missing videos and figure out how to repair ornery copying machines. Prepared teachers are not stressed out, and neither are their students. Their carefully organized classrooms are places all children want to be.

Starting the Day Right

And now, the dawn of a new day. It is hard to begin with the toughest item first, but there are no better ways to add minutes to the day than the following:

• Get up 15 (or more) minutes earlier every day. These 15 minutes are just for you and doing something you love: reading an inspirational passage, adding notes to a diary, scanning lesson plans for the day to make last-minute adjustments, writing a letter to someone you care about. These few self-centered minutes are vital to your well-being and the launch of a great day. (Note: No more snooze button.)

• Because you have already laid out your wardrobe for today, continue your morning routine—exercise, shower, eat breakfast, and then jump into your clothes. The time saved by having a morning routine eliminates stress from things like no clean clothes or misplaced shoes.

• Leave for school so that you arrive at least 15 minutes before the mandated time (more may be needed, but this is a reasonable start). These minutes can be precious, especially because the fewer people there are at school, the fewer interruptions there will be to a great start in the morning.

If you are fresh out of college, this routine of getting up early may be a bit horrifying. College days seem to start at noon and end around 2:00 a.m. Teaching does not operate on that time schedule. It is easier to awaken refreshed when you go to bed looking forward to the new day. This may require some attitude adjustment, but if you begin by turning in earlier at night while thinking of a great start tomorrow (like hot coffee, the morning news, a walk or a run, or petting the dog), this new routine becomes revitalizing. Starting each day by engaging the heart and mind in an activity you love affects your attitude for the rest of the day.

Arriving at school is stress free when everything is already set out for teaching. You have time to

- Review your lesson plans.
- Add notes to the board as needed.
- Check again on students with missing, late, or makeup work.
- Sort handouts and papers you graded and recorded last evening so they are ready to return to students.

Avoid having students in class before school unless they are working on assignments or need extra help. Although they may love to visit, this preplanning time belongs to you. The same is true with colleagues who just like to talk. Their chatter soaks up needed preparation time. Politely agree to meet them at lunch or on a break.

Bell-to-Bell Instruction

Bell-to-bell instruction means that the lesson starts as the bell rings and ends as the bell rings for dismissal, with no empty or disruptive minutes. Organized teachers

- Greet students as they enter the room.

- Start class as soon as the bell rings by having students begin their bell work while you take roll, hand out papers, get a lunch count, and complete other duties.

- Begin the lesson according to the lesson plan phases. Pay close attention to the approximate time allocation for each phase to maintain instructional pace.

- Adjust lesson content to meet the needs of students while also recalculating the minutes left for teaching. Typically there are just a few students who do not understand, so a minilesson can fill in gaps as other students begin their independent work. If a majority of students are confused, you may need to revamp the entire lesson.

- End the lesson five minutes before the bell or before transitioning to a new subject with a closure activity that reviews what has just been taught and learned, summarizes key ideas, or requires students to write a reflection note. The end of class is not disengagement time but, rather, debriefing time.

- Maintain student engagement until dismissal. Do not allow students to halt learning by closing books, getting out of their seats, wandering around the room, or chatting about anything other than the day's learning. Every minute in class must be filled with learning to manage time wisely.

- Prepare for the next lesson. If you have a self-contained classroom, students can get out the next textbook or assignment and open to the correct page before they go to recess or elsewhere. If a new group of students is coming in, use these minutes to rethink and prepare again for instruction.

Although you may have only three to five minutes to regroup between subjects or student groups, use those minutes to self-evaluate the lesson by asking yourself the following questions:

- How did this lesson match the time allotment?
- How well did this lesson achieve the desired outcomes?
- What must be
  - Added to make the lesson better?

- Omitted because it is unnecessary?
- Presented differently to reach all learners?
• How was the pacing of the lesson? Was it slow because of
  - Difficult concepts?
  - Student absences?
  - Students' inadequate background knowledge?
  - Lack of continuity due to various interruptions?
• Did it finish too quickly because of
  - Inadequate planning?
  - Poor materials?
  - Insufficient explanation?
  - Lack of challenge?

If you time each lesson perfectly, you can meet all essential teaching goals, resulting in fewer learning gaps for students. Remember that if you think you are running short on time and so decide to skip teaching vocabulary, you may add confusion for students when they try to understand a concept or passage. On the other hand, if you spend too much time discussing vocabulary, you never move through the entire lesson and students may never know why the vocabulary was important. The minutes spent on each phase of the lesson vary each day based on the content, but the basic phases remain constant.

From Hours to Weeks of Smoothly Running Instruction

After one hour of teaching is perfectly planned and goes off flawlessly (or pretty much so), teachers soon discover that half-days run well, and then full days. This success then extends into weeks and eventually into units or projects that last over a longer period of time. Last-minute surprises don't vanish, but experience, practice, confidence, and skill solve many problems.

Complacent or self-satisfied teachers rarely teach their best. Reaching and teaching every student every day is a tremendous responsibility and requires dedication to student achievement. What makes the effort fun is that it challenges creative skills and keeps teachers alive with enthusiasm. Lackadaisical teachers ... lack! Energetic teachers energize.

Videotape Your Teaching

Videotaping and critiquing your teaching and delivery can be a scary proposition, but you gain excellent information when you study yourself in action. Analyzing and evaluating yourself as you teach and interact with your students as they learn can improve instruction. If you are taping the lesson yourself, a camera set up in the corner of the room with a wide-angle lens will suffice. The advantage of working with a peer is that he can adjust the camera to follow you as you move around the room. A mentor or other trusted colleague may be willing to videotape for you, especially if you are willing to return the favor. Certain facets of teaching can only be understood upon careful review; viewing the videotape is the best way to gather unbiased information. Videotaping your work over time will help you see and document your growth and changes in teaching practices. Above all, the videotape is to help you study your teaching, not to offer home entertainment or to serve as a vehicle to ridicule yourself, your teaching, or your students. Figure 8.1 provides a form for critiquing your instruction.

Homework: Lessons That Extend Outside the Classroom

Homework is practice time that extends learning from the classroom to home and back. The premise behind homework is that practice and repetition engrain knowledge and skills to create a stronger foundation for the next phase of instruction.

Many students (and their parents) struggle with homework. Some students have no suitable place to do homework; others have parents who do not care if their children complete homework or who are not home to supervise the work. Still others have parents who would like to help their children, but language or educational barriers and work schedules prevent them from

Figure 8.1	Video Critique Form

Name:
Date Videotaped:
Date Reviewed:

Instructional Practices	Notes

Presence
  Mannerisms
 	
  Posture
 	
  Appearance
 	
  Poise
 	
  Voice	

Classroom Movement
  Students seated; orderly,
  planned movement
 	
  Smooth classroom
  procedures
 	
  Proximity (moving about
  room)
 	
  Classroom awareness	

Oral Presentation
  Clear, concise instructions
 	
  Appropriate questions to
  match lesson
 	
  Questions that enrich
  thinking	

(continued)

Figure 8.1	Continued	
Instructional Practices		**Notes**
Instructional Techniques Scaffolded instruction (I do, we do, you do) Clear directions Multiple modalities addressed (visual, audio, kinetic) Learning goals clear Check for understanding Lesson with clear and focused beginning, middle, end Instructional pacing evident		
One aspect of your teaching that went very well: One aspect of your teaching you would like to improve:		

doing so. Homework, if it is tackled at all, is often incomplete or copied from friends. Grades are earned on others' work, and only poor test scores signal that a student has not learned the material.

When class time is well spent and all phases of the lesson are taught, homework exercises solidify skills. When homework is hastily assigned with insufficient background, it may set students even further back, because either they refuse to complete it or they do it with such confusion that misconceptions become difficult to correct. Well-planned homework saves time; confusing homework or homework that is simply busywork saps time from the next lesson.

Suggestions for Smooth Transitions

Carefully guard every minute of the day by engaging students with learning. Smooth transitions allow for change of pace and focus with no disruption. Many of the points discussed in earlier chapters related to classroom management and other aspects of instruction are pertinent. Here are some suggestions for smooth transitions:

• Use name tags for roll, hot/cold lunch count, calling on students randomly.

• Have a seating chart handy for checking attendance.

• Place baskets, stack-ups, boxes, or bins for turning in work by subject or period in a location that is convenient for students as they enter or leave your room.

• Post the schedule of the day (and maybe the week or month) so students know the order of subjects, special events, and special classes such as physical education or computer lab.

• Post goals and objectives by subject area so that students know what they will be learning during the day and so they can refer to it at the end of the period or day as they reflect on "What I have learned."

• Have books already on the desk and open to the correct page to begin work immediately after recesses, lunch, and pull-outs.

• Write page numbers, directions, and other information on the board so that directions are given once and students can then refer to a written source for any information they missed.

• Absolutely refuse to repeat responses to questions already clearly answered. This may take intensive self-training as students learn the importance of good listening.

- Absolutely refuse to answer questions when you are otherwise occupied or the questions are off-task.
- Write bell work or other assignments—a journal assignment, a quick write, or other activity—on the board so students are immediately engaged in learning. The topic should link to the expected learning; it should not be random writing that serves no purpose.
- Use envelopes or folders with each student's name listed for turning in money, book orders, and other special items. As students enter the room they can grab their envelope, place important items inside, and then put it in a designated spot. This procedure eliminates lineups at your desk, money scattered around the room, or papers left in mysterious piles for you to determine the significance of later.
- Have baskets where students who have been absent can pick up homework, assignments, worksheets, and other materials missed while they were gone. This arrangement also avoids the need to dig through piles to find missing assignments. Writing students' names on each item before placing it in the basket simplifies the procedure.
- Establish procedures so there is no confusion about expectations for student movement around the room.
- Express friendliness, calmness, and joy so that students know you are pleased that they are in your class.

I entered a classroom of 1st graders just as a guest completed a lesson. As the speaker finished the presentation, she handed the students a paper to color in their "free time." A student piped up, "Free time? We do not have free time." A second added, "We are always learning. We will not have time to do this unless you give us a learning objective." Finally, a third chimed in, "Can you tie this to our lesson framework?"

If you really want to know the importance of using time wisely and having clear, focused goals and objectives, just ask a 1st grader!

Closing Advice

Regardless of how you try to divide and multiply the day, there are only so many minutes available. The best way to remedy missing-minute madness is to make every available minute meaningful and productive. Procrastination and frustration are minute-munchers that can be tamed with planning and organization. The extra minutes you gain in the morning by waking up a little earlier set you up for a successful, less stressful day. By using the time guidelines presented in this chapter and then streamlining classroom instruction, you can recover missing minutes.

It is also essential to be mentally set for teaching. Waiting to copy a worksheet for classroom use at the last minute guarantees that 17 other frantic teachers will be in front of you in line at the closest copying machine—which is about to malfunction. Then the counselor will stop to ask you a pertinent question about a student, a parent will call, your administrator will ask you to stop by on your lunch break, and a student will race up and smack into you, causing a bloody nose. All of this and the school day has only begun! Every day brings surprises, but early arrival and preparation help you to be ready for these challenges. The end of the day is the same. Extra minutes that permit you to unwind, reflect, and prepare for tomorrow are extremely valuable.

9

Every Moment Counts: Strategies for Student Engagement

— • • • —

You now have created detailed, engaging lessons and units in which each minute is precisely organized and put to good use. Now you must ensure that students attain desired learning outcomes. To do this, you must know how and when to check for understanding and then make adjustments for ongoing success. Students learn in different ways, and so you need multiple strategies and activities to reach all of them, especially when you are teaching new and challenging concepts.

Gone are the days of teachers feeding information to students and students mindlessly regurgitating it. The complexities of education and the expectations for learning are too high to assume the recipient understands the material. Although assessments provide scores related to learning, engagement strategies inform you immediately as to what students know or do not know, where they need extra instruction or reteaching, and which ones are ready to move on. With teaching that includes a variety of techniques that maintain student attention and strategies that expose understanding, you never have to face that horrific moment when no one appears to have learned anything.

The Challenge

One of the essential goals of any teacher, whether a novice or a veteran, is to reach each child and help him become a capable, independent learner. Noel Morton moved to my district with several years of teaching and administrative experience. The district was in her hometown, and she was eager to return to the classroom.

Three of Noel's 3rd grade students were young boys that I had tagged as the "Sad Eye Boys" from previous observations in earlier years. These children were struggling academically and personally. What a gift they received when they were assigned to Noel, a master of knowing the academic level of every student in every subject, right down to the concept being taught on a particular day. Her room is organized so that students are constantly engaged in learning. For example, during reading, one group is with her, while four other groups work individually or as a team to complete pre-assigned work. Students with questions ask a more able peer for help, and the peer assists with obvious pleasure and then returns to her own work. For an hour and a half, students are in a steady learning mode, totally focused on their work. After a recess break, they excitedly return for more.

Every student receives direct instruction from Noel and does independent work and practice to improve skills. They each know the learning goal and Noel's expectations, because these are posted on her board, have been repeated orally, and are also written on each assignment. The absolute proof that students know their learning goals comes from simply asking them what they are doing and why. No matter which student I asked or at what point during the lesson, they always knew what they were learning, how it applied to past learning, and how it would support what they were to study next. In fact, when I was too curious and wanted to ask additional questions about their learning, they would become nervous and quietly tell me, "I am sorry; I have to get this assignment done," and then refocus themselves on their work.

Each day that I was in Noel's class, I studied the "Sad Eye Boys," and each day their eyes brightened until they became the glowing eyes of eager, confident learners. Her attention to every student and every detail of each lesson developed students' confidence and competence. With this love and perceptive instinct, plus organization and determination, Noel's hard work rewards every student every day.

Lessons Learned

Do not think that all of this classroom productivity arose magically simply because Noel was experienced and had an excellent background. Although there was definitely "magic" in her room, it was the result of hours and hours of preparation and planning. It is common for me to run by Noel's school on my 5:30 a.m. jog and spot her car in the parking lot with the lights of her room turned on as she prepares for the day. Great teachers possess devoted commitment to student achievement and the belief that all students can learn and succeed. Those teachers have a lasting effect on students and make a positive difference forever.

Daily Questions and Journal Prompts

One way to engage students is by getting to know them personally. A Student Interest Inventory like the one in Appendix B contains questions that help teachers relate to each student as an individual. Students can write short answers directly on the interest inventory form for easy reference throughout the year. Expanded responses may be written in a journal or binder that is ongoing and large enough for a year of writing, which keeps all of the responses in one location that is easy to collect, read, respond to, and return. Students may respond to one or two questions as part of the daily bell work, or the questions can be used as a writing prompt. Here are some additional examples of getting-to-know-you prompts for the first days of school:

• What is the most exciting event you have studied about in United States history? Why?

• After you read a favorite book, do you prefer to write about it or talk about it with a friend? Explain.

• In science last year, from which experiment did you learn the most? Describe three of the facts or concepts you learned.

• Draw a picture of your family. (This one is good for young students who can't yet write.)

Lesson plans can include a daily question or journal prompt to grab students' attention and, when used as bell work, to draw them into the lesson and hold them accountable. Here are some examples:

• What are the three most important things you remember from yesterday?

• What is one question you have about yesterday's lesson?

• What is one question you have on the topic of _____?

• What was the easiest part of yesterday's lesson?

• What was the hardest part of yesterday's lesson?

• When you see the word _____ [either a term from a prior lesson or a new term for today], what do you think of?

• If you were to define _____ [key term] for a younger friend, how would you explain it?

• Draw a picture of _____ [key term/concept] from yesterday's lesson.

• What predictions can you make about today's lesson based on these terms?

• How do _____ and _____ link together to help you better understand _____?

Prompts can also connect to the learning from yesterday or last week, as in this example:

• Draw three geometric figures that we discussed last week. Tell which figure would be best suited for the shape of a playground for preschool children, and explain why you chose this shape.

Having students answer questions that require reflection and explanation reinforces understanding while making you aware of what students do and do not know. Some teachers may argue that this type of writing is for English class, but students have much personal insight that they want to share. Writing to their teacher is one way to demonstrate their learning. As for grading, it is your decision as to how simple or complex to be.

Of course, you want students to use correct grammar and spelling, tools essential for developing good writing. To quickly assess student writing, glance through the responses and jot short notes to students about their thinking and learning, or write a question to which they respond to increase communication. Grades may be optional, but make it clear that this writing is very important and that you expect a thoughtful response. As students truly begin to own their learning, it will not be the letter grade or point value that motivates them but, rather, your respect for their thinking and ideas.

If your students are unaccustomed to writing or have never before been asked to do reflective writing, you should be prepared to answer questions such as these:

- What is the primary goal of reflective writing?
- How long is long enough?
- How much weight is placed on getting the main idea or a right answer? Or is it creative, reflective thinking that you want?

If you really want your students to trust you with their writing and their thoughts, you cannot seek one single right answer. If students know there are multiple possibilities for correct responses, they will be more willing to take chances on learning and sharing ideas.

- How often will students write short responses?
- How often will students write extended responses?
- How often will writing be collected, read, and graded?
- What percent of the total grade, if any, is a result of these writing assignments?

- What will happen if students write but the answer does not demonstrate that they "get" the concept?
- How will you challenge students to expand thinking when their answer indicates they "get" the concept?
- Will student writing be confidential? (Yes!)

Although writing offers an excellent opportunity for reflection and evidence of student engagement, it also pinpoints misconceptions in learning and identifies concepts that need reteaching. Frequent writing means you can discover problems early in the learning, when they are much easier to correct. Writing is one way to capture student thinking before, during, and after the learning. Writing is engaging, and engaged students learn.

This may be the first experience that your students have ever had with writing, and they may need you to cheer them on and celebrate their ideas and insight. If some students initially struggle with writing, it is most likely because they have never been encouraged to express their thinking in this way. Time, patience, and positive feedback will increase their confidence and skill. Research shows that when students can write about a topic or a concept, they develop a far deeper understanding. Regardless of the age of your students, you will be astonished at their analytical and evaluative abilities.

As students ask questions about writing, you can respond by reaffirming the multiple benefits of reflective writing (see Figure 9.1, p. 148) for sample questions and answers). Your positive attitude toward the benefits of writing will motivate students to write and then to write more. Writing is an enlightening way to engage students. As always, plan ahead for students who have forgotten their writing notebook by having them write on a separate sheet of paper (staple it into the notebook later). When you collect the notebooks, be certain that you read and return them quickly so that the continuity of writing and reflecting remains connected and essential to learning.

Figure 9.1	Student Questions and Teacher Responses on the Benefits of Reflective Writing

Q Why do we have to write this? I did the problem [project, homework, assignment].

A Writing helps clarify the learning, and it also guides the teacher in creating the next lesson. Student input and ways of responding help teachers understand learning and thinking.

Q We have never written in math [or science or social studies or English] before. Why are we doing this now?

A Writing is a great way to solidify learning of concepts.

Q Is this for a grade?

A Of course it is for a grade. Life is a grade. People are always getting "marks" based on output and performance. [Whether or not it is actually graded or a point value is assigned is up to the teacher.]

Q This is science. Does spelling [or grammar] count?

A Of course it counts. Good spelling and grammar are important. Throughout life people judge others on their writing and make serious determinations about intelligence based on this. Writers write in all subjects.

Q We do not even write in English. Why are we writing in history?

A [This one is scary.] Writing is so important for clarifying understanding; and reading what students have to say is fascinating. [Avoid discussing the practices of other teachers.]

Q Do you really read all of these?

A [Students will know the answer because of teacher notes scattered throughout the entry. Speed-reading entries is fine. Just add a quick note here and there to show personal interest.]

Other Strategies for Student Engagement

True engagement, when every student is on task and learning, reflects quality instruction. One of the reasons teachers enter the profession is because they love the subject or the age group. Now they have the opportunity to motivate students to become enthusiastic learners, by sharing their knowledge and enthusiasm. The rest of this section describes various strategies to use to keep students engaged in learning.

Quiet signal. Students must know when to talk and when to listen. Teachers must never talk over students, just as students must never talk over their teacher. Hand signals such as one finger in the air, count down (5, 4, 3, 2, 1), or echo claps (teacher claps a pattern and students respond with a pattern) are effective quiet signals. A bell or chime works well, too.

Bell work. Whatever form it takes—writing in a journal or completing a challenge problem, model, or short activity that grabs students into learning from the moment the bell rings—bell work is an ongoing procedure for the start of each class, each day. All assignments must be meaningful and engaging, with students held accountable for completion.

Homework. Students who struggle with turning in homework need guidance, not simply a failing grade. Talk privately with the individual students who do not complete homework, and together decide on an action plan. The plan may include the following:

- Time spent with you for extra help at lunch
- A call home to help establish a regular homework time and conducive conditions
- Homework makeup time after school
- A modified homework plan that meets learning goals but is shorter or less complex, matching the task to the learner

All assigned work must be so valuable and engaging that no student would consider not finishing it.

Note cards, Popsicle sticks, or other student identifiers. As described in Chapter 6, cards or sticks with students' names written on them can be used for calling on students in random fashion. It is easy to fall into the ritual of asking a question and then calling on the first person with a hand in the air. This approach allows you to move on with the lesson, but it also leaves the false feeling that all students "get it," when perhaps the only one who did was the person whose hand flew up. To hold all students accountable and engaged in learning, follow this procedure:

- Ask the question.
- Pause for at least five seconds (wait time).
- Randomly draw a name from the sticks or cards.
- Call on that student to respond.
- Call on two or three more students randomly to extend the learning and to increase the thinking of the entire class.
- Put the sticks or cards back into the pile so that students know that they may be called on again.
- After students reply to a question, follow the response with "Are you certain?" "Class, do you agree?" or "Tell me more." These questions force students to evaluate and justify their thinking and expand their response.

You can also have students write the response on paper, a white board, or a note card for further evidence of student engagement and understanding.

For some students this engagement procedure will be new. Older students, especially, have learned to sit quietly and fake attentiveness because the first person to raise a hand is the only one ever called on. Observe students carefully and then ask, "Can I *prove* that every student was engaged in the learning?" If the answer is yes, you have engagement.

Share with a partner. Ask a question, have students share their response with a partner, and then randomly call on students to share their mutual or best response and thoughts with the class. Sharing with a partner is a procedure that improves with practice as students learn to remain on task even with a friend. When students know the purpose for sharing with a partner (generating thinking to develop a response) and when the partner time is carefully monitored (not too long!), they stay engaged in thinking about and focusing on the discussion question. Again, you have accountability in action.

Thumbs-up. Pose a question, wait, call for a response, then have students signal with a thumbs-up gesture if they agree with the response. Check to see who agrees or disagrees, and then call on several students to explain their thinking.

Show your cards. Ask the question, get one response, and then have students hold up a colored card to indicate their agreement or degree of understanding:

- Green = "You bet!"
- Yellow = "I think that will work."
- Red = "No way" or "I don't get it at all."

Repeat, rephrase, or reformulate the question until all students indicate understanding (by holding up a green card or by sharing a response). This quick assessment assists in determining configurations for learning groups.

Learning groups. Divide the students into groups based on their understanding of certain concepts. Provide a minilesson or other assignment for each group. The green group begins work on an assignment—perhaps a more challenging one than the rest of the class because the students understand the concept; the yellow group works together to respond to or solve some similar questions or problems as a team while you oversee their progress; the red group receives individual help and guidance from you—for example, with a small-group minilesson on key learning points. These students might also work with a more able learner who helps them grasp the new concepts. Attending to learning difficulties early on increases understanding while decreasing the need for reteaching.

Dry-erase boards. Give each student or pair of students a board, an eraser, and markers. You or a partner in each pair poses a question, and the students respond on their dry-erase board and then hold up their responses to check for understanding. Students of all ages love the dry-erase boards, and they provide an efficient and effective way for all students to practice new skills or concepts.

You can purchase dry-erase boards or make them yourself. Simply get white or colored construction paper or tagboard (8½″ × 11″ sheets) and slip the sheets into page protectors. Students can write on the page protector with dry-erase markers. An alternative is to purchase a sheet of melamine from a lumber yard and ask an employee to cut it into the desired size for individual boards. You can also ask the shop teacher to help, or borrow a saw and cut your own. Teachers of younger students recommend smaller boards for their students because they are easier to handle; of course, the boards should be large enough to provide adequate room for responses.

Think-pair-share. Pose a question. Have students think about the response and then share with a partner. Individuals then share with the class. This strategy is especially helpful for second language learners or struggling students because chatting with a partner is less stressful than addressing the entire class. Good partners provide clear feedback that supports the learning. Verbalization with a partner also allows students to clarify understanding while improving oral language skills.

Write-pair-share (Marzano, 2007). This strategy is similar to think-pair-share, but students write a response first and then pair with a partner to share. This approach saves time when students are called on because they have a written response ready.

5-2-1 (Bonwell & Eison, 1991). Lecture, demonstrate, explain, or direct the lesson for five minutes. During the next two minutes, have students share the learning with a partner, practice on their own (on something you can easily see, such as a dry-erase board), or write in their journals. Then allow a one-minute debrief for students to share their ideas with the whole class or a partner. Listen carefully to identify points that require reteaching or to determine that the class is ready to move forward. Repeat 5-2-1 throughout the lesson.

Knowledge blocks (modified Cornell notes). Have students fold a piece of binder paper into four parts. The quarters may be divided evenly or may be of varying sizes, depending on the requirements of the assignment. The first section can be for notes from the teacher; the second, for key vocabulary terms; the third, for questions; the fourth, for jotting down the homework assignment. The possibilities are endless. See Figure 9.2 for examples of how to set up knowledge blocks.

Figure 9.2	**Examples of Knowledge Blocks**

Example 1 (lines indicate paper folds)

Class lecture notes	Student questions or responses
Key vocabulary	Homework and practice

Example 2

Questions I have before reading	Responses found in text
Predictions about the text	Verification of predictions found in the text

Example 3

Vocabulary term	Dictionary or class definition
Draw a picture of the term	Term used in a sentence or question

Note card vocabulary (Blachowicz & Fisher, 2006). Teach key vocabulary terms or concepts, and then have students write the new words or concepts on a note card in large letters (felt-tip pens work well for this). On the opposite side of the card, have students write a definition or draw a picture that illustrates the vocabulary word or concept. Students can also indicate the chapter in the book or page number where the term is used or the topic to which it applies for reference.

Punch a hole in the upper-left-hand corner of the card and attach it to a large ring or tie with ribbon. Add new vocabulary cards to the ring throughout the year. The ring keeps vocabulary current and available for reference and review. The activity also teaches students that learning key terminology is not a one-shot effort but an ongoing task. This automatic review expands knowledge of the terms through repeated encounters.

Quick write. Offer direct instruction and then have students write as much as they can about the topic in one minute (or 20 seconds) on a note card, on a small piece of paper, or in their journals. A timer displayed where students can see how much time remains really makes them concentrate on the task, and many times they write even more. The small paper or card can be used as an exit pass or a passport or as a fast review.

Exit pass or passport. On a small piece of paper or a note card have students write a short explanation, summary, or list of questions pertinent to the learning of the day during the last few minutes of class. Students hand this in when class ends. This information provides insight for planning future lessons.

Timer. Use a kitchen timer, display an overhead timer, or download a chalkboard timer from the Internet. Estimate the amount of time that it will take for most students to complete a task, then shorten that time a little. Providing too much time invites disengagement. Give the instructions, provide the expectations, point at the instructions that are already written on the board, set the timer, and allow students to work. A timer engagement strategy may be used for small groups of students or for students to work individually.

Assignments That Count

Make all assignments valuable, enriching, and purposeful. Problems often arise when activities seem pointless to students or are deemed as busywork. Younger students may complete the work simply to please their teacher. Older students grow more cynical and may refuse to complete meaningless drivel. Here are some points to remember:

- Students want to be challenged but not overwhelmed.
- Students do not want senseless tasks that are below their ability level.
- If you assign work, you must do something with it (grade it, discuss it, have students share it with partners).
- Explain, clarify, and then challenge students to think while completing the assignment.
- Avoid repetitive, mundane worksheets that require lower-level thinking.

It is important to remain aware of students and the way they interpret and comprehend what is being taught. For many years, in many schools, teachers have taught children—or at least boasted that they had taught them—only to have them fail a final test at the end of the grading period with no recourse for improvement. The typical reaction was "I taught it, but they didn't learn." The real question is, Did the teacher really teach or simply go through the motions of teaching?

All students, regardless of age, are children, and they want to learn and succeed. They do not always fully appreciate the value of their learning at the moment, but none of them starts each day hoping to fail. They come to school being the best they can be at that instant in time. Teachers have the power to bring success to each child in their educational care.

Closing Advice

Great teachers ignite students' desire to learn by motivating them and sharing their own enthusiasm and passion for developing and enriching young minds. It is impossible to stress enough the responsibility that goes with teaching and the importance of excellence. Teachers who apply themselves conscientiously by promoting success for all and by appreciating the uniqueness of each learner help their students gain deep understanding. Students are counting on diligent teachers who are patient and filled with expertise to guide them toward learning success.

There will be tough days, days when you are tired or flat-out exhausted. But there will also be days of exuberance and elation. Some expressions of thanks from students and parents may come tomorrow, others may come years down the road, and still others will never be revealed except deep in the heart.

10

Questions to Activate Thinking and Ignite Learning

• • •

While teaching lessons, you have made sure students are engaged by using a variety of engagement techniques; checked for understanding before, during, and after instruction; and explained, demonstrated, and retaught as needed. Afterward, you have reflected on the lessons, the responses of students, and what needs to be done next. It's time now to think more deeply about the kinds of questions that are a key element of good instruction—questions that verify understanding and then move students onward to thinking beyond the levels of recall and understanding.

Although textbooks supply questions, many of those questions do not advance student thinking into application, evaluation, analysis, and the creation of products, projects, or performances. The type and quality of questions teachers ask can guide students to deeper thinking by incorporating abstract and complex reasoning.

It is only when students can take their learning and use it in multiple ways and situations that you can be certain that they really "own" their learning. Ownership indicates what students know and can do now—and how they will be able to manipulate and use their knowledge in the future. Savvy teachers know the value of great questions that divulge knowledge and drive the next steps of instruction.

The Challenge

Stan was in kindergarten, and as he told us about the letters he had learned that day, his voice slowly began to fade as he leaned over into his dinner and slipped into sleep. We gently woke him up and asked if he would like to go to bed. "I can't go to bed yet," he replied, and then he picked up his fork and began to eat once more. Soon he slumped forward again, and I awakened him and repeated my suggestion that he go to bed. "I can't," he insisted.

On the third snooze, I gathered him into my arms, lifted him up, and headed for his room. As he awakened, large tears tumbled from his eyes and dripped onto my arm. "Mom, we have tests tomorrow. I can't go to bed yet. Mrs. Doughty said we were to eat a good dinner and go to bed at 8:00. It's only 6:30. I won't know the answers if I go to bed now."

Lessons Learned

Stan wanted to please Mrs. Doughty, his kindergarten teacher, by doing exactly as she had asked, knowing that heeding her advice would mean getting everything right. Your students are much the same. Every one of them wants to be "smart," to know the answers, and to succeed. As a teacher, you teach the subject and help students advance, but you are also a model for learning and achievement. Students trust your words and believe in you just as you believe in them.

Bloom's Taxonomy

Bloom's taxonomy (Bloom et al., 1956) is a hierarchy of questions formulated to increase higher-level reasoning. *Lower-order* questions are those that require students to *recall* basic knowledge and information and *understand* the concepts of the learning. *Higher-order* questions are those that require students to *apply* knowledge from the learning; *analyze* the facets or parts of the learning; *evaluate* the learning and how components work together; and *create* new understanding with synthesized learning.

By beginning with questions at the lower end of Bloom's taxonomy, you can check that students "get" the main ideas of the topic or lesson; these questions reveal fundamental understanding. When you are confident that students have a solid foundation of understanding, you can pose higher-order questions to move students to think beyond the concrete and into the abstract. Abstract thinking is sometimes referred to as "reading between the lines," or understanding the unwritten or unspoken implications of information. Literal thinkers may search extensively for "hidden" words that supply the answer. Abstract thinkers realize that they must dig inside the concept to uncover the answer. All questions should be designed to help clarify understanding, pique curiosity, promote a desire to learn more, and transport students to deeper thinking.

Some may say that it takes vast stores of background knowledge to move students to the upper level of Bloom's taxonomy. These people have not been in classrooms with young students. Give students a few clear, pertinent facts, add some information and a couple of ideas to ponder, allow a little think time, and students develop wonderfully profound responses. They really want to know "why" and "how" about each marvel of learning that greets them. Part of instruction is fanning student curiosity throughout the school years so that it can continue to burn throughout life.

• • • • • • • •

Students come to school believing that they are invincible and can learn and do anything. Hand a 3-year-old a crayon, and she can write (it is we who cannot read). A 4-year-old can grab a book (even if it is upside down) and read it to us (even if the storyline is made up or recited from memory). Students can count, add, subtract, and perform other math skills until speed and automaticity become more important than having fun with learning and working at a comfortable pace.

Children must know and be able to do so many things. However, by forcing them into a mold designed with time constraints and limited possibilities, teachers and schools sometimes snuff students' curiosity and their belief that they are capable of learning. Use tests, academic standards, and other educational demands, to fill your lessons and your students with the wonder of discovery and learning through enthusiastic, creative instruction with questions that enhance thinking and reasoning.

Some students arrive with a preconceived notion of not being good at math or English or physical education. In these cases, well-formulated questions and activities that probe thought and require application of knowledge and skills can negate this notion.

Questions to Promote Learning

Good questions are part of ongoing instruction and assessment for learning, and they serve one of two purposes. They (1) support and promote student learning and achievement, and (2) enable teachers to evaluate and analyze student learning and achievement.

Good questions do not demean students but, rather, allow them to demonstrate their knowledge and degree of understanding. This does not mean it is OK to accept wrong answers or to further misconceptions. It does mean it is important to encourage students to think and rethink. A repertoire of good questions includes the following:

- Entry-level questions that provide an initial foundation for and of learning

- Deeper questions that move students beyond preliminary understanding to reach new levels of comprehension
- Well-formulated, engaging questions that have focus and direction and that expand thinking

Students can memorize multiplication tables and respond to questions on timed tests in a flash; however, it is the application of this knowledge in real situations that makes this mathematical skill valuable. Possessing knowledge is the beginning; being able to use knowledge is a life requirement. Good questions can move students from rote responses to thoughtful applications of knowledge.

The reverse is also true. Give children an application problem for multiplication with no knowledge of how to multiply, and although they may arrive at an answer, they can experience great frustration and confusion along the way. Good teachers provide the background knowledge and reinforce the skills so that multiplication makes sense.

To create great questions, use the effective questioning strategy in Figure 10.1. The levels of questions in the figure relate to Bloom's taxonomy.

As a junior in college and after several changes, my daughter Allison finally settled on health ecology, a major that covers most medical fields. After the initial foundational classes, she hit the first really tough course, anatomy and physiology, which required extensive memorization plus deep understanding of body structures, movement, and functions. She did not mind the studying, but she worried about having missed some courses that would have provided her with greater background knowledge.

Each day in class, one student waved her hand after every question the instructor posed and then gave long, convoluted answers. Although this student dominated the discussion, Allison was not intimidated. She realized that the student had probably taken previous classes that supported her knowledge and that soon she would know all of those answers and more. Allison did not give up or

Figure 10.1	Effective Questioning	
Level of Question*	**Possible Types of Questions**	**Suitable Assessment Techniques**
Recall	• Recalling key points of information • Drawing on knowledge from past learning • Identifying basic similarities and differences	• Two-column matching • Multiple choice (with no more than two or three choices for younger children) • True/false with no explanation required for the choice • Fill-in-the-blanks from a word bank • Dry-erase boards/thumbs-up • Narrative essay
Understand	• Examining information and changing it to another format (e.g., facts into a poem, figures into a graph) • Providing examples (e.g., amphibians include____) • Recognizing patterns • Explaining events using structures such as cause/effect or if/then	• Short-answer responses • Graphic representations • Completing graphic organizers • Dry-erase boards/thumbs-up • Narrative essay
Apply	• Completing a procedure, such as a science experiment that extends understanding • Selecting specific information, format, or steps and using them in unfamiliar situations	• Selecting the most efficient from two or three graphic organizers • T-chart—solving problem on one side, explaining the steps on the other • Short-answer response • Solving a problem in more than one way • "How to" essay

Figure 10.1	Continued	

Level of Question*	Possible Types of Questions	Suitable Assessment Techniques
Analyze	• Examining each of the parts to determine how it fits the whole • Differentiating between important and unimportant facts • Building connections based on information provided • Identifying misconceptions or misinformation • Organizing—building sequential connections based on pieces of information	• Venn diagram • Written responses based on information from text or problem • Selecting a problem-solving method by determining the relevant and irrelevant information • Graphic organizer that compares pieces of information • Expository essay • Fill-in-the-blank response based on analysis of information
Evaluate	• Verifying ideas and concepts for consistency with information presented • Judging projects, products, and performances based on certain criteria • Confirming information between sources	• Venn diagram • Comparison of key components, texts, explanations, or events • Short answer with proof from text • Expository essay • Determining the most efficient procedure based on certain criteria and determining any errors in conclusions drawn
Create/Synthesize	• Designing projects, products, or performances based on learning • Developing solutions to problems or situations • "Inventing" projects, products, or performances based on novel insight or solutions	• Projects, products, or performances based on learning • Narrative and expository essay • "How to" essay presenting new ways of thinking • Experimenting to generate new information • Revising and editing an essay to expand ideas, intent, and impact

*Level of Question based on Bloom's taxonomy.

feel inadequate but realized that more learning would increase her understanding.

All teachers have Allisons in their classes—students who sit, listen, and increase their knowledge daily. They might not respond frequently, but that does not mean that they do not have excellent thoughts and ideas. Engaged students who want to learn hold themselves accountable. When students recognize what they really know and can do and then work to know more, teachers have ignited learning.

Question Starters

Using the different categories of questions shown in Figure 10.1 is one way to shift students to higher-level thinking. Here are some "starters" for each category:

- *Recall* and *Understand* Questions
  - What?
  - Who?
  - When?
  - Where?
  - How many?
  - Why do you think ____? [Any question in this form indicates that all answers are acceptable because the response is an opinion.]
- *Apply* Questions
  - Why?
  - What if _____?
  - How would you do _____?
  - How would _____ affect _____?
- *Analyze* Questions
  - What might happen if _____?
  - How are A and B alike/different?
  - If you were to _____, how might the outcome change?
  - Why is it essential?

- How does A distract from B?
- What does the author [scientist, problem] omit that is necessary for understanding?

- *Evaluate* Questions
  - How does A relate to B?
  - According to _____, why does _____?
  - What problems are inherent when _____?
  - If A is replaced by B, how do the results change?
  - Based on _____, why does _____?
- *Create/Synthesize* Questions
  - Build _____.
  - Draw, create _____.
  - Construct _____.
  - Write _____.
  - Design _____.
  - Perform _____.
  - Demonstrate _____.
  - Draft _____.

There are many more questions suitable for desired learning outcomes, but these provide a framework. Make active, constructive thought part of every lesson. Do not think that because students appear to be struggling with a concept or a skill that they do not also have a brilliant idea brewing. Often students know the information but the teacher has not yet asked the right question to reveal understanding. "Explain your thinking," "Tell me more about _____," "If you thought you knew how to _____, what would you do?" are just a few of the questions that promote reflection and extend responses.

Younger students are often eager to blurt out answers, so spread the opportunity to answer to all students. Older students tend to withdraw, and although there may be one hand constantly waving, call on all learners each day to verify learning. Complacency does not beget active learning.

Questions for All Ages

It is often easier to engage young students who are bubbling with enthusiasm and curiosity about everything. Somewhere around 4th grade, school gets harder. Those who are struggling may fall further behind and, without intervention, become lost in learning. They need someone like you to swoop in and reroute them to success by asking carefully crafted questions that assess their understanding and restore their confidence.

Junior high school is another academic dividing point for many students. Often students at this level have been cut loose from self-contained, tightly knit classrooms and now have a variety of teachers and classes and a blossoming interest in just about everything except academics. Although few groups of students are more demanding to teach, young adolescents think openly and are untainted by cynicism and total discouragement. Students this age are just plain fun when their curiosity and desire to learn are piqued by good questions.

High schools are full of students exploding with knowledge and zest for learning as well as those who have retreated into the deepest, darkest corners of the classrooms to melt into invisibility. Engaging instruction with inspirational questions is critical.

I clearly remember my first cheating episode because it was also my last. I was in the 1st grade. You must be shaking your head in wonder and saying, "Cheating in the 1st grade? How can that be?"

We were learning to spell the names of colors. We had practiced, read, written, and spelled again and again, so the test should have been simple. As I was writing my answers, I drew a complete blank on *purple*. What were the letters? What did that word look like?

The colors were displayed on a large poster behind me, and I tried to will those words through the back of my head and onto my paper.

If sweat and agony had been sufficient to call the word to mind, the correct letters would have flashed onto the page.

As time was running out, an incredible thought hit me. "I know where to find the answer!" I stealthily pulled my box of crayons from my desk, yanked out purple, and carefully copied the letters onto the test paper: V-I-O-L-E-T. I had succeeded—I had spelled *purple*. Mrs. Fisher would be so proud of me.

As Mrs. Fisher walked around the room gathering our papers, she leaned over and whispered, "I know what you did." I recognized that she was referring to the test and cringed. I knew that I had disappointed Mrs. Fisher, and I was not going to do that ever again.

It was much later, probably when I actually learned to spell *purple*, that I understood the significance of my action. My teacher could have handled my cheating in many ways, but her words were all that was necessary—"I know what you did." This experience initiated my awe of teachers and my belief that they knew absolutely everything. It impressed upon me the need to listen and study for success and not to rely on cheating.

Creating Assessments That Support Students and Inform Teachers

Excellent instruction organized around effective questions benefits both students and teachers. With excellent instruction, students can think and apply their learning at all levels of Bloom's taxonomy, achieve desired learning outcomes, and gain the ability and background knowledge necessary for further learning. Questions and responses give teachers information about students' knowledge and insight gained from lessons, richness of thinking and understanding, and preparedness for future learning. Proof of this student achievement comes from feedback from reliable assessments.

Assessments are tools for gathering information about student understanding that can then be used to guide future instruction. Assessments also check and verify the quality and effectiveness of instruction. Good assessments answer these questions:

- What do students know?
- What are students able to do with their knowledge and skills?
- What is the proof/evidence of what they know?

After deciding on an assessment that is best suited to gathering the desired information, teachers must know how to use the results. This information leads to more questions:

- How do teachers enrich student knowledge to advance learning?
- What do teachers do when students have not yet learned or only partially grasp a concept?
- How do teachers enhance the learning of struggling students so that they can achieve at the highest levels and gain equal footing with their peers?

One of the most important jobs of teachers is determining what kind of assessment will best identify what they need to know about student learning and their own instruction.

Formal and Informal Assessments

Schools use many kinds of *formal* and *informal* assessments. Formal assessments are carefully designed and include state or national tests, a test from a book or textbook, and other examinations created by the classroom teacher or teaching team that produce a score or a grade. These assessments are most often an end product, a way to culminate learning in a particular area. Informal assessments are used when checking for understanding before, during, and after a lesson. They reveal what students know and can do and indicate areas that require additional assistance. Because the feedback is immediate, teachers can make adjustments during instruction, such as using a different strategy, repeating and reviewing with more examples, or breaking students into smaller learning groups based on degree of understanding. Informal assessments are ongoing throughout the lesson, unit, and year. Figure 10.2 (p. 170) divides assessment into formal and informal categories to clarify the differences.

In addition to the examples listed in Figure 10.2, here are other kinds of informal assessments:

- Signals—agree, disagree, unsure; thumbs-up, showing a card to indicate degree of understanding (green, yellow, red)
- Dry-erase boards—whole-class response so teacher can assess understandings and misconceptions
- Entry passes, exit passes—quick student jotting that the teacher uses as feedback for designing the rest of the lesson or future lessons
- Hands-on projects—models, replicas, designs, illustrations, or drawings
- Games to assess learning—bingo, homophone rummy, concentration games in which all learners participate
- Teacher notes from observation—written after class to help determine next steps in teaching
- Interviews with students and parents concerning learning and progress
- Student-led conferences—student explanation to parents of the significance of grades already posted, as well as information about learning strengths, goals, and areas that need work

Some teachers have misconceptions about assessment. Some believe that assessment is *only* done at the end of the lesson or unit to generate a grade or other evaluation measure. By waiting until instruction on a particular concept is complete and then assessing the learning, teachers often discover that it is too late to prevent or repair deep misconceptions or confusion or to help students reach the desired learning outcomes.

Often schools test students and then do nothing with the data other than record a grade and move on. Students are too valuable to justify continuing this unproductive practice. When you receive test results, use them to improve teaching and learning.

Figure 10.2	Formal and Informal Assessments	
Formal		**Informal**
Tests	Small quizzes	
Diagnostic test for placement	Diagnostic test given during an oral lesson (to check understanding, decoding skills, ability to infer)	
State and national tests	Quizzes that prepare students for format, question type, expectations of large tests	
Formative subject-area assessments for a grade—end of chapter/unit exam	Subject-area assessments that focus on learning what students know so that teaching can be adjusted	
Summative subject-area assessments for a major grade—nine-week or semester exams	Subject-area assessments that focus on finding gaps in learning so that future lessons can be designed accordingly	
Formal writing that is graded and has specific learning goals—research paper, poetry compilation, essays, lab reports	Journal writes, quick writes so that students can verbalize their learning; may be short or quite extensive	
Performances—plays, demonstrations, musical productions	Short, quick responses to demonstrate learning or skills and to determine next steps	
Products and projects—dioramas; science fair projects; formal displays such as castles, forts, and other structures	Figures created to display the understanding of concepts	
Notes made on report cards or cumulative records	Anecdotal notes taken as the teacher listens and observes students engaged in learning; checklist with set criteria on which the teacher notes degree of proficiency	
Checklist in rubric form—used to determine a grade on a project or product based on predetermined criteria	Checklist on which the teacher checks student performance against a rubric to check progress	
Group projects that end with a formal product and grade	Individual guidance on small, in-class projects	

Figure 10.2	Continued	
Formal		**Informal**
Portfolios—large, formal compilation with several entries that demonstrate knowledge and growth; course or school requirement for a grade, promotion, or graduation		Classroom portfolio in which student assembles work based on own choice of what to enter or not enter; may include student self-evaluation of work in sections or for entire portfolio; if graded, student has input into the grade

Another common occurrence with test results is to use letter grades to label students who do not achieve and then to relegate them to remedial programs from which they rarely emerge. Remediation is, well, remedial. Struggling students need enriched, fully fortified instruction with the unwavering goal of attaining the necessary skills and knowledge to become proficient.

Assessment Formats

Assessment may be written, oral, visual, or in a performance format. Much formal assessment is written, using multiple-choice, essay, and short-answer questions or a checklist or a scoring rubric to indicate degree of proficiency. Formal written assessments provide proof in writing of what students know and do not know based on the questions included on the test. Informal written assessment includes responses given on whiteboards, notepaper, sticky notes, a graphic organizer, or a formatted assessment sheet (a quiz!) based on what the teacher has taught. Quick writes, for example, are written by students during a lesson to reflect their learning or to list questions about today's lesson to guide the next steps of instruction. Exit passes are written at the end of the day's lesson to guide future instruction.

Oral assessments may be student responses in whole-class discussion, responses as students interact in small-group discussions, or responses they share with a partner. In any of these situations, the teacher listens to responses to ensure student understanding and then adjusts as necessary by repeating, paraphrasing, reteaching, or emphasizing key points of the lesson. With oral assessment it is crucial that all students have the opportunity to speak and share ideas so the teacher gains a complete picture of classwide understanding.

Performance assessments may take place in classes such as music, theater, or shop. Students actually execute their skills while the teacher assesses strengths and determines areas that need further work.

Visual assessment includes observing students as they respond to questions and then providing feedback on their answers. This format uses many of the engagement strategies discussed in Chapter 9. In some cases, visual assessment may simply involve studying the nonverbal cues of students, such as expressions of joy or frowns of frustration.

Some assessments are a combination of written, oral, performance, and visual. A dance assessment that includes written questions about specific dance moves, a short oral explanation of the dance itself, and then a performance critiqued through a scoring rubric is an example.

There are many specific types of assessment, each of which has advantages and disadvantages. Figure 10.3 describes what different assessments look like and how they are best used.

It is essential to select a type of assessment that will produce the desired outcomes. Great assessments in the wrong format do not correctly evaluate the attainment of specific desired outcomes or present data that are valid and meaningful. For example, if you want to know if students can explain and demonstrate knowledge of key artistic techniques, a multiple-choice test is worthless. In this case, an assessment that includes short-answer explanations and drawing examples of each technique provides the necessary feedback to know how students are processing and using the skills taught.

When planning major projects, products, or performances, create a scoring rubric that delineates your desired outcomes and expectations for learning. Building a diorama can become

Figure 10.3	Characteristics of Assessments		
Type of Assessment	**What It Looks Like**	**When/Why Use It**	**Drawbacks**
Multiple Choice	Offers three or four choices; replicates format of most state and national exams.	Quick; easy to score.	Good, plausible "wrong" answers are hard to write; guessing can be good enough. Avoid "all of the above" or "none of the above" as choices to avoid confusion and to pinpoint key idea.
True/False	Offers two choices—true or false.	Quick; easy to score; easy way to check recall and remember information.	Guessing can be good enough; time-consuming to create equal number of true and false statements.
Word Bank	Several words are listed; students choose appropriate word from the bank.	Quick; easy to score; easy way to check recall and remember information, especially definitions.	Guessing can be good enough; students might select one wrong term and then completely miss all other answers.
Fill in the Blank	Sentence has a blank space for missing information; students fill in.	OK if you are just checking a few things and the answers are fairly finite.	Can be difficult to grade if possible answers are numerous.
Graphic Organizer	Outline is provided with some information present and other information completed by student.	Good for helping students learn to select important information; helpful for ELL and special needs students because it is guided.	Depletes paper supply; time-consuming to find or design the perfect organizer.

(continued)

Figure 10.3	Continued		
Type of Assessment	**What It Looks Like**	**When/Why Use It**	**Drawbacks**
Matching	Two columns contain words or phrases that students match to indicate correct relationship (e.g., date and event; term and definition)	Easy to create; quick to score unless students draw lines from Column A to Column B.	One incorrect answer can throw off the whole matching process; guessing or elimination can be a problem.
Retelling, Rephrasing, Paraphrasing	Information is provided, and then student repeats, including the key points.	Easy way to check one-on-one or small-group understanding; for whole class, written responses use class time more efficiently.	Including all students takes time and may cause other students to lose focus if done orally; requires strict adherence to wait time to get all students to respond.
Short Answer	In response to a question, students answer in just a few sentences.	Easy to grade if questions are clear and have only one correct answer.	Poor handwriting can be a problem; some students are afraid of writing.
Constructed Response	Students follow a pattern when responding to a question and support answers with direct information from the text; precise scoring guide accompanies the question.	With guidelines, easy to grade; bulleted answers make responses quicker to score; must make sure that response matches scoring guide.	Poor handwriting can be a problem; some students are afraid of writing; some students are used to "anything goes" answers and do not know how to "prove" answers with textual evidence.

Figure 10.3	Continued		
Type of Assessment	**What It Looks Like**	**When/Why Use It**	**Drawbacks**
Essay	Students respond with longer, in-depth answers, drawing extensively on their knowledge.	Moves students into upper levels of Bloom's taxonomy—apply, evaluate, analyze, create; allows students to exemplify knowledge.	Poor handwriting can be a problem; some students are afraid of writing; tedious to score without a clear scoring guide; difficult to grade consistently against all other papers.
T-Chart	Student writes the problem above the T, solves the problem on the left, explains the steps (with terms, not numbers) on the right.	Allows students to exemplify knowledge; pushes higher-level thinking; if students can solve and explain one problem, they can probably do many more; helps pinpoint where students are making errors. Great for math.	Poor handwriting can be a problem; time consuming if too many are assigned.
Models, Replicas, Illustrations, Designs, Dioramas	Uses building blocks, tools, other materials to construct models of learning.	Shows student ability to manipulate objects for a number of reasons and end results.	Needs to be one child's construction to determine individual ability, which can be expensive and time consuming.

hours of busywork if students do not know details for scoring, including desired size of the finished product, design type needed, features to be included, time period to be replicated, and labeling requirements. (Perhaps dioramas are better as drawings and written explanations than as expensive models.) A good rubric clarifies what the teacher is expecting as a finished product and how each part of the project will be scored. There are no mystery grades with a well-defined rubric.

My mother's friend was earning her degree in counseling and needed an agreeable person to take a wide variety of tests. I was selected for the task.

I love tests—the challenge, wracking my brain, and the ideas and learning that result. One of the tests I completed was a national exam that all sophomores in my state were required to take. During the next school year, I repeated the same exam I had taken for fun during the summer. I was amazed at all the things I knew the second time that I did not know when I had taken the exam just a few months earlier. My brain had stored questions, hoping that my experiences would provide the answers.

I always encourage nervous test takers with this story and remind them about the marvelous brain that is working for them. In addition to all of the things we know, there are many other things we know with a little probing. "Test anxiety" is a foreign term to me. I never met a test that I did not think I could conquer.

Acting on the Results

When assessments reveal disparities among students, it is important to act accordingly. If students in Group C are ready to move on, send them on their way with independent work that is challenging yet doable. Students in Group B, who almost have the idea, will benefit from a minilesson that moves them to independence. And students in Group A may require a complete reteaching, using new strategies that target the missing learning.

Although at first it will feel time-consuming and overwhelming to make so many modifications and adjustments in lessons, eventually you will move seamlessly to help all students learn. Developing this skill transforms you from novice to intermediate and finally to exemplary teacher.

Portfolios and Assessment for Learning

Portfolios are another way to assess learning. They provide an ongoing collection of sample assignments and exams that teachers can use to study student growth over time. The same collection assists students as they self-assess their improvement as well as identify areas that require further study.

The first step in using portfolios is to determine their purpose. Do you want a collection of student work that

- Indicates mastery in specific areas or in several areas?
- Reflects growth during a unit of study?
- Reflects growth in a total year-end compilation?
- Is designed by you with required entries in a particular order?
- Is designed by the students, who also determine the order and select the entries?
- Includes student reflection on growth and personal determination of work selected for the portfolio?
- Is gathered by you with entries saved and used as exemplars in future years of teaching?
- Is graded or ungraded as a whole?
- Is graded by the student, by you, or by faculty committee?
- Ends with the school year?
- Is carried over from grade to grade?

Decisions about the purpose of portfolios are complex but need not complicate implementation. By establishing portfolio goals and including students in the process of selection and self-evaluation of individual pieces of work, the bulk of the responsibility is placed on students. Study Figure 10.4 to decide how portfolios will work best for you.

I used portfolios for an 8th grade English class that were simple compilations of essays and other writings that students placed in a folder. They chose 25 pieces and self-evaluated them from best

Figure 10.4	Portfolios	
Student Generated		**Teacher Generated**
A collection of student work is organized in a particular way with clear guidelines and a scoring rubric.		A simple collection of student work is taken from a variety of assignment types.
Students are involved, including possibly self-evaluating their work and selecting entries.		The teacher randomly selects work based on what she feels is important; includes proficient assignments along with those that needed more attention.
May require additional materials, such as notebooks or binders; more complete collection may take extra storage boxes or file cabinets.		Papers are stored in a file folder or other readily available place.
Students have ownership because they make decisions about contents.		Students are not involved in entry selection, and so process can be less time-consuming.
Students can review their work to understand growth and comment on what they have learned and where they need further study.		Students may never see the complete collection to understand their growth in learning. Portfolio may become a dumping ground if students do not review their work to determine advancement of skills.
May be passed to next teacher and then added to year after year.		May be a single class or teacher assignment; the teacher may return the folder at the end of the term or year or keep it for future reference.

(#1) to lowest ranking (#25). Each student created a table of contents with comments on the various artifacts included and what the student saw as strengths or areas that needed improvement. The final portfolios were impressive, as they revealed growth through self-evaluation. I hosted a Student/Parent Portfolio Night at the end of the year at which students and their parents sat down and pored over the portfolios together.

The next year my friend Georgette Olsen, a math teacher, said, "What a great idea!" and we added math portfolios. She created a questionnaire for parents to complete as they read their child's papers, which provided us with additional feedback as to how parents interpreted student improvement. Later, science, art, and computer teachers joined in. Imagine the delight of parents on Portfolio Night as they moved through five different portfolios, including a digital portfolio from the computer lab. I do not know who gained the most from this—we five teachers, the students, or the parents.

Closing Advice

Variety in types of questions and assessments provides a broad picture of student learning. Including a little of everything from throughout the term can be a good plan, especially because students need to have skills in taking many types of assessments with many different kinds of questions. Designing the right questions and selecting the right assessments produce informative results for future planning.

Always ask these questions:

• What do I want my students to know as a result of this lesson?
• What are the desired learning outcomes?
• How will I know that my students know?
• What will I do with my students who know?
• What will I do with my students who do not know?

Combining instruction with meaningful questions and assessments informs you about your teaching and students about their strengths and areas of concern in learning. By determining the learning goals before instruction and continuously checking for understanding during lessons with short, incremental assessments, you know that students will be fully prepared for their final assessment.

11

Grading, Student Achievement, and Student Self-Evaluation

• • •

You have worked hard to make sure that you have taught all lesson concepts and skills; provided time for students to practice and review; adjusted lessons, implemented strategies, and varied activities to reach all students; and incorporated all levels of Bloom's taxonomy into learning. The assessment results for your students reflect your desired outcomes. Now for the really tough part: assigning a grade.

Although many people may believe that grading is easy—as in right or wrong, pass or fail—assessing student learning is a complex undertaking. A grade indicates a score on a particular assessment on a particular day with certain concepts and skills emphasized. That might mean good day, good test, good score or grade. A rough day might produce quite different results.

Assessing students and assigning grades are generally a requirement of teaching. The largest portion of your day, however, will be spent with ongoing brief assessments that support students as they progress through learning and guide your instruction as you work to reach every student every day. In the back of the mind of an excellent teacher, questions are constantly brewing: Why am I teaching this concept? How does learning this information help students? How do I advance students who "get it" immediately? How do I help those who do not? This type of continual self-evaluation turns potential learning into academic success.

The Challenge

Learning, athletic experiences, and a love of competition drew my son TW into teaching and coaching. After three years as a junior varsity basketball coach, he changed schools and became the varsity coach. Every year he has had wonderful players who are fine students as well as dedicated athletes. Observing TW as he interacts with his team demonstrates much about good teaching. Basketball is an in-your-face sort of sport with such intensity and emotion that it is difficult not to become upset. Over time and with practice, he has learned to adjust his style, words, and approach depending on the situation and the player at that exact moment. This effort has had a powerful effect on his players.

During practice and games, TW talks to his players one-on-one and as a team. When they make mistakes, he explains how to solve them as he draws diagrams to illustrate his intentions. His players go through repeated practice until their skills are fine-tuned. Although the desired outcome of every game is victory, these players also develop leadership skills and confidence that will carry them through other facets of school and life. Growth, improvement, and self-reliance are products of good coaching as well as good teaching; they are important contributors to students' lifelong success.

Lessons Learned

All students have great potential. Sometimes it is quite obvious and easy to draw out. In other cases it is buried deeply and needs continuous effort to be revealed. Good teachers, like good coaches, have the ability to turn potential into reality by teaching, sharing, demonstrating, reteaching as necessary, and always believing in the possibilities of success in every child.

Why Grades?

Assessing student work pinpoints student strengths as well as areas that need improvement. This feedback guides adjustments in your instruction while you work to move the entire class along at a pace that guarantees that all students attain the desired outcomes. Although this achievement may seem impossible, it is an educational goal and expectation.

The expectation is present whether you are teaching 20 to 30 students at the elementary level—which is tough enough—or 200 or more students at the secondary level. Not only is it necessary for you to study and plan so that you teach everything students need to know; you also must carefully evaluate the learning progress of each student to ensure success now and in the future. You have assumed the incredible responsibility of teaching all students.

Culminating Grades

Scores on state or national examinations are culminating marks. They reveal knowledge and understanding but are rarely used as a tool to improve instruction or to fill in learning gaps for students. The results of these exams are reported to schools, but not seeing the question or problem makes it difficult to determine exactly why items were correct or incorrect. Grades at the end of the year do approximately the same thing. Perhaps the next teacher will check the grades and review test scores, but quite often the letter grades are recorded and forgotten unless the student must repeat a course because of a failing score.

Nine-week and semester grades often lead to the same reaction. The teaching is done, the learning has been assessed, and so it is time to move on. This attitude is especially unfortunate when a struggling student continues with no one who acknowledges strengths or helps the student overcome areas of concern.

Great teachers assign grades as required, but they also study these marks to formulate future lessons that will help all students reach and exceed proficiency. Because most school systems require grades, consider them as a guide but also use them to inform and improve your instruction.

Ongoing Grades

The majority of classroom grades result from ongoing assessment. When you know the desired outcomes for each lesson and unit, planning always begins with the end in mind (Covey, 1995; McTighe & Wiggins, 1999). Every strategy, activity, lesson, and teaching moment leads to the achievement of these outcomes. The insight gained from assessment shapes future instruction as you ask questions such as these:

- Which concepts need reteaching?
- Which students need enrichment lessons?
- Which students need challenge lessons?
- How can students advance to even higher levels of achievement?
- How can the allotted instructional minutes be best juggled to meet the needs of all learners?
- What changes are needed to meet the learning needs of diverse students?

Fortunately, sometimes all students "get it" at pretty much the same pace, which allows you a momentary, worry-free breather. At other times, even duplicating yourself many times over would not enable every student to be reached. Nevertheless, persistence, dedication, preparation, and belief in students will pay off.

Sometimes teachers have to retrain students to look at growth in learning rather than simply a letter or a number on an assignment. Many students and parents believe that the grade is what matters and the learning is just a side effect. With my students,

I learned to "hide" the grade inside the assignment so that they had to read through my comments and corrections to discover and thus better understand their score. After some training, they began to enjoy this challenge while also studying the notes I had written to improve their work.

Assigning Grades

Grading student work requires a multipronged analysis: distinguishing learning from effort, lack of learning from frustration, and overachievement from underachievement. By analyzing the subject area, the learner, the prior knowledge base, the way information was presented, and the assessment format, you can make instruction more effective.

Personal bias must also be considered. Students are just kids; some are easy to be around and are always ready to please, and others are struggling and do not mind causing their teacher to struggle too. The struggling students need extra positive attention, different teaching strategies, a variety of learning opportunities, practice with the concept or skill, and patience from a teacher who believes in them.

Teaching and grading are not finite activities. Educational decisions are based on facts such as scores, attendance, participation, and student self-assessment, but they also require looking at each student as a unique individual. Sometimes the events in students' lives make education a low priority for them. Personally knowing and caring about students increases the probability of helping them.

Great teachers track every aspect of learning and adjust lessons as they teach. With mini-assessments along the way, when the time comes for the "big assessment," these teachers are already aware of probable results—all students passing lessons that were taught and learned well; not all students passing if there was need for review and additional instruction.

When teachers think of assessment as a grade on their instruction and a grade on students' learning, the complexity of grading becomes obvious. Teachers cannot start on page 1 of a book and move through it page by page and expect all students to read along and understand the same things at the same time. If teachers were not critical to the learning process, students could learn on their own, and they would never need a teacher to guide and challenge them.

Learning Versus Grades

As you assign grades, ponder these questions:

• Which is more important, the learning and improvement or the grade?

• How many chances does a struggling child get with the learning?

• Are you certain that your students know or do not know what you have taught?

• Are your lessons designed so that all students can achieve the desired outcomes?

• Are the assessments designed to evaluate student learning based on the desired outcomes and the quality of lessons taught?

• How can you deal fairly with every student when each student is so different?

• How does each grade, each comment, and each interaction encourage student growth?

Self-analysis and reflection plus input from trusted colleagues and students will support and improve your grading procedures.

Keeping Students in the Know

Periodically let students know their grades, assignments that are missing, areas of strength, and areas of concern. Late work and makeup work present problems if students and teachers are not on top of it all. When students are updated about their progress, there are no surprises when grades are posted. Here are some considerations to keep in mind with regard to late work or makeup work:

- Are there extenuating circumstances for the late work or makeup work?
- Is redoing a failed or missing assignment beneficial to the student and learning?
- Are you up-to-date with all grading so that students know how they are doing, what they are missing, and areas on which they need practice and review?
- Is a zero or a failing grade on the assignment the best way to improve learning?
- Does 100 percent or an *A* mean there is no room for growth?
- What can be done so that all students achieve at the highest levels?

When I began teaching, I accepted no late work or incomplete work. I did not grade papers without names. I strictly adhered to these rules, and they worked. My students' parents supported my rules; consequently, students made the mistake of not completing an assignment only once. It seems like eons ago that everything was turned in complete and on time.

During my last teaching round, I found that no rule worked perfectly unless it also came with some flexibility. When children are raising siblings, there is no food in the house, Dad drinks, Mom sleeps all day, and the family is totally dysfunctional, how can a teacher hope that a student will remember to write and turn in an English essay?

Leniency is not the answer in all cases; being strict is not the answer in all cases. Being as fair as possible, knowing your students personally, communicating with your students and their parents or guardians, and always attempting to provide the best instruction are behaviors that serve you well.

Student Self-Evaluation

Assignments and assessments reveal a wide range of information about student learning and achievement of desired outcomes.

You can discover even more when you ask students about their learning with questions like these:

- What was easy in this unit/test? Explain.
- What was hard in this unit/test? Explain.
- What was confusing in this unit/test? Give an example.
- How confident did you feel about the material taught?
- How much did you study?
- How much effort did you exert in the learning?
- How much information was new?
- How much information was review?

An interesting question that often prompts the best responses: "What did you study that I did not ask on this test? Share your knowledge." Allowing students to share this knowledge intensifies your understanding of their learning, thoughts, and study habits and provides an outlet for their ideas on significant concepts of personal value. Such questions give students the opportunity to demonstrate learning and can easily be added to an assignment or assessment.

Another way to learn about students' competence is to have them indicate understanding as they work on the assignment or assessment. They solve a problem, show their work, and then respond by choosing one of the following options to show their degree of confidence:

- Solved the problem—it was easy because ...
- Solved the problem—unsure, but I think this is right because ...
- Solved the problem—I guessed because ...
- Could not solve the problem because ...

This activity provides useful information about students and their degree of understanding. If students write that they guessed and they get the answer right, you are at a different point in instruction than if the students say it was easy but provide an answer that is confusing or incorrect.

Other ways to increase knowledge of student learning and establish a base for self-evaluation is to have students do the following:

- Show their work—math and science
- Explain in complete sentences—English, social studies, or any other subject
- Demonstrate—science, fine arts, speech
- Perform—art, music, physical education
- Produce a project or product—shop, art, science, English
- Explain in an oral presentation
- Combine any of these to more clearly reveal knowledge and skill

A written self-evaluation completed at the end of a lesson, unit, project, or performance reveals much about the student's work, planning, and organization as well as the process undertaken to achieve the desired learning outcomes. Here are questions that promote reflection:

- What was the most valuable information gained during this unit of study?
- How will you apply this knowledge in other areas?
- What do you wish I [the teacher] had done differently when learning about _____?
- What more would you like to know about _____?
- What are you still unsure about?
- What else should I [the teacher] know about your learning?

It is also important to examine assessment results for each student on each concept or skill to determine proficiency in the material being tested. For example, on a math test a student receives the following scores: 4 out of 5 answers correct on addition, 3 out of 5 answers correct on subtraction, and 1 out of 6 answers correct on multiplication. The total score is 8 correct out of 16, or 50 percent, which is a failing grade. However, this student is actually doing well in addition, is fairly proficient in subtraction, but needs additional practice on multiplication. Using this information, the teacher can avoid reteaching concepts that the student already understands and reassure the student that there is only one area that requires emphasis. What a boost for a positive outlook on learning!

My first experience with student self-evaluation came during an English course in my second year of college. We received a lengthy reading list and were told to come to class every day. We were told to take (not pass) a midterm and a final, and then we would receive credit. Those seemed like odd course requirements, but I was 19 and believed my professor knew best. I read the books and I came to class, but we never discussed our reading. Some of us chatted, the professor's favorites played games with him, and I decided that was just how college English classes operated.

The midterm questions were basic recall on the 10 books we had read. Although picking out details like "What color was the door?" was not my forte, I survived. The final was quite different. It contained more than 100 questions that required detailed responses from the 20 books we had been assigned. The last question was a self-evaluation one: "What grade do you want?" It was not what did you *earn*, not what did you *learn*, but what did you *want*. Of course, I wanted an *A*.

As I left the room, I noticed the group of favorites. Not only did they not have a test to complete, but they were shuffling through the tests of classmates, smirking at answers and at the self-evaluations. Although I learned nothing about English, a love of learning, or the beauty of reading and writing from this class, I did learn other things, such as fairness, organization, goals for all students, and the defeated feeling that comes from poor instruction and confusing expectations. Teaching, learning, assessment, and self-evaluation involve so much more than just a grade.

Examining Assessment Results

It is also important to study each question and look at how many students answered correctly and how many answered incorrectly to determine the validity and reliability of the assignment or assessment. If all students got the answer to a particular question correct, it may indicate that you did a terrific job teaching or that the question was too easy or not really thought-provoking. The same is true if all students miss a question. You must ask

- Was it the instruction?
- Was it the question?
- Was it the question format?
- Were there errors or confusing terminology that affected responses?

By tallying the right and wrong answers to a particular question, you can learn about your instruction, the assessment, and your students. On multiple-choice questions, note how many students chose A, B, C, or D to determine the quality of the question and the response choices and to analyze why students got an answer right or made mistakes.

Closing Advice

Grading and evaluation procedures are a topic that could be extended into an entire book. There is simply so much to know about teaching and learning. The more you read, learn, and apply new ideas and strategies while studying the actions and reactions of your students, the more proficient you will become at teaching and the more successful your students will be.

Use the grades and scores from assignments and assessments to evaluate and improve instruction. Check for understanding throughout lessons and units and use this feedback as well. This approach eliminates surprises or sad endings for you or your students when it is time to record a final grade. All students want to learn and succeed, and, as their teacher, you can provide the positive force that transforms their potential into reality.

12

Final Notes for
Teaching Success

· · ·

Even with meticulous planning and excellent preparation, the flow of student understanding can adjust the direction of the lesson. Jamie Billingsley is a first-year teacher whose morning starts with busy 1st graders with needs and behavior issues that cannot be met in the mainstream classroom. What Jamie lacks in experience, she makes up for with her desire to ensure that every child succeeds. By October, as is typical of first-year teachers, Jamie suffered a series of colds, bits of the flu, and some natural exhaustion, along with an outburst of pimples. As she worked with John on math one morning, Jamie tried several approaches to get his attention, but everything failed. Finally, she asked, "John, what's wrong? Why can't you focus today?"

John replied, "Miss B., I'm scared!"

"Why? Tell me so that I can help you."

"Well, on Monday you had three pimples on your forehead. On Tuesday, I saw two on your chin. And now I see three more starting. What's wrong?" asked John.

Jaime was a little surprised by John's straightforward comments and his fear; on top of that, her ego suffered a small blow.

But she quickly regained her poise and responded, "All right. Let's solve this problem. How many pimples did you see on Monday?"

"Three," said John.

"And on Tuesday?"

"Two more."

"And how about today?"

"Three!" shouted John with glee.

"OK, let's see. 3 + 2 +3 = how many?"

"Hmm. 3 + 2 = 5, and then I'll add 3 more. 8!"

"That's great thinking. Now let's build that pattern." And John and Jaime used blocks to create the equation, rearranged the numbers, regrouped, and even added more "pimples." Jaime was able to seize an uncomfortable moment for her and manipulate it into a teaching moment that engaged John in learning the math lesson.

Teachable moments fall everywhere during the day. Savvy teachers are ready to grab hold of each question, each concern, and try to solve it so that learning can proceed. Jamie recognized that John was under some sort of stress and that it was keeping him from learning. Fortunately, he was willing to share the problem, allowing Jamie to address it and transform it into relevant instruction.

One of the most exciting aspects of teaching is that every day offers new ways to learn and grow. Although you can never be completely prepared for every possible question or event, your positive attitude, strong professionalism, and communication techniques will carry you far. Next year, as you reflect back on this one, total amazement at the wonder of working with young minds will energize you for another magical adventure. Here are some tips to keep in mind to help you become a savvy teacher from the outset.

Professionalism. Always be professional in your attitude, behavior, clothing selection, and overall appearance and cleanliness. Regardless of the size of the school where you teach, in a village or a city, students and parents are looking to you as a positive role model.

Advance preparation. Always be prepared with lessons that enrich, backup materials that support the lesson, and understanding of all the learners in your care. No student wants to fail. Students are counting on their teacher to make a difference in their learning now and forever.

Advice. Seek help and advice from colleagues to ensure that students succeed. Colleagues can help you improve lessons, assessments, and learning, and learn the "secrets" of the job. It is essential to learn as much about teaching as quickly as possible. Find a trusted colleague to support you as you begin your career.

Attitude, communication, and interaction. No matter what the day brings, remain positive. Even on the toughest days, students are counting on you. You will find a way to reach and teach every child. It is also possible to have a cordial relationship even with the most trying parent or colleague.

Make open-house evenings, parent–teacher conferences, and other special events opportunities for stakeholders to learn about you and your expectations and for you to learn about them. Continue to learn and grow by taking at least one or two classes per year; attending professional conferences, seminars, or workshops; and joining an education-based organization, especially one with excellent publications. Other ideas include subscribing to at least one education-based periodical, teaching or team-teaching a class/workshop for colleagues, and collaborating with teachers you trust and who will make you better at the job.

● ● ● ● ● ● ● ●

There is no career more fun or important than teaching. What a wonderful way to make a difference in the world!

Maryjo Dufurrena has taught for several years, beginning in rural Nevada and more recently teaching 5th grade in town. Although she is an experienced teacher with great talent, Maryjo invited me into her classroom for discussion, observations, model lessons, and feedback. After the students and I read *The Polar Express* and discussed key features (who, what, when, where, why, how come, and lessons learned), I shared another story that reflects the main points of the writing lesson. I told them about the time that I baked 12 dozen cookies in preparation for a frosting project with a group of patients who have Alzheimer's disease. Unfortunately, an error in communication meant that no one came to the frosting session. So, I frosted the cookies, put them on plates, and headed down the hallway of the hospital. As visitors approached, I asked if they liked Christmas cookies. Positive responses gave me the freedom to give them a plate of cookies and to wish them Merry Christmas. Within 15 minutes, all my cookies were bestowed upon surprised guests.

At the end of my story, students responded to the key features and we discussed the importance of each in making a complete tale. With this in mind, students wrote their own stories about a time of surprise, kindness, and learning. As they wrote, Maryjo and I circulated throughout the room, asking questions to help students clarify their writing and assisting with grammar and encouragement. Our interaction and enthusiasm ignited the imagination of the young writers and was revealed in their papers.

At the end of the session, the students left their papers for us to read and said goodbye to the crazy cookie lady. A paraprofessional in the room approached me and said that my story and enthusiasm for each student's story gave her the guidelines and courage to write about her own mother, who had Alzheimer's disease.

As a teacher, you will affect many lives in a powerful way. Every word, every lesson, and every scrap of feedback and enthusiasm can influence everyone in your classroom. Maryjo even told me that "I now know how my attitude elevates or deflates my students and their responses. I didn't know that writing could be so much fun."

A few months later, I was observing a different teacher's classroom. As Mrs. Dufurrena's students filed into art class, they greeted me as "the writing teacher." And then they told me how much they love writing.

Affirmation of your work arrives from different sources at the most interesting times. It is not the praise or the accolades that enhance your instruction, but all the little things in between. Small expressions of thanks, smiles, personal writing samples for you to read, and radiant beams of success on the faces of students as they gain confidence and competence are the best affirmations.

Year Two Is Near!

News flash! Your second year of teaching will be far easier than the first. You will have experienced the lessons, developed the atmosphere of your very own classroom, and faced and overcome many challenges and daily surprises. But no year is ever simple. Students change, textbooks change, colleagues and administrators change—all of which keep you learning and growing.

An uplifting occurrence you can look forward to is when first-year teachers tap on your door and ask for advice. Although you may look seasoned and wise, new teachers will not realize that you are also just beginning your career, and the struggles and adventures of the first year of teaching will be fresh in your mind as you share newfound expertise.

Great teaching takes time. As with anything done well, practice, study, trial runs, and ongoing adjustments bring future success. The longer you teach and the more experience and insight you gain, the better prepared you will become for every teaching moment. Have fun! Teaching is truly a wonderful adventure.

Appendix A:
Lesson Plan Template

Time Allotment (Minutes)	Lesson Phase	Details
Phase 1	**Introduction**	
5	Set a purpose. Introduce the topic with a grabber and information to get students thinking. Make the learning relevant.	
Phase 2	**Foundation**	
5–10	Check on previous learning. Clarify key points of the coming lesson, including standards, goals, and objectives, building background knowledge and key vocabulary.	
Phase 3	**Brain Activation**	
5	Ask questions; clarify; provide additional background knowledge. Perhaps include a brainstorm activity on the topic to check learning.	

(continued)

Time Allotment (Minutes)	Lesson Phase	Details
Phase 4	**Body of New Information**	
10–15	Build background knowledge, lecture, and introduce key new points of understanding, correcting misconceptions. Read text; complete whole-class problems; conduct class discussion.	
Phase 5	**Clarification**	
5–10	Provide sample problems and situations. Pose questions to move students toward independent work.	
Phase 6	**Practice and Review**	
5–10	Students work with teacher and whole class, in small groups, or with a partner to clarify learning.	
Phase 7	**Independent Practice**	
10	Students practice on their own. Begin homework. Struggling students get additional practice.	
Phase 8	**Closure**	
5	Connect the lesson details together. Answer questions and respond to whole-class difficulties.	

Appendix B:
Student Interest Inventory

• • •

Name: _____

Class: _____

1. What is your best subject in school? Explain why.

2. What is your toughest subject? Explain why.

3. What is one goal that you have for yourself in school? Describe it.

4. What is one goal that you have for your life? Describe it.

5. Describe your brothers or sisters, cousins, or other relatives.

6. Describe the characteristics of your best friend.

7. What is the best vacation you have ever taken, and why?

8. What is the best book you ever read? Summarize it and explain why you liked it.

9. What is the best movie you ever saw? Why did you like it?

10. Who is your favorite musical group, and why?

11. What sports do you like? Describe the one that you like best and why it is best.

12. What are your hobbies? Describe one.

13. What is the best school program that you ever participated in, and why?

14. What is the best school project that you ever created, and why?

15. What was the best moment that you have had so far at school?

16. If you could go anywhere in the world, where would it be? Explain why you want to go there.

17. What is your favorite food (color, pet, season)? Tell more about it.

18. If you could meet anyone on the world, past or present, who would it be, and what would you want that person to tell you about?

19. If you could change places for a day with anyone, who would it be, and why?

20. If you could meet the president (an actor/actress, sports star, historical figure), what questions would you ask him or her?

21. If you could choose to either go on a cruise to Hawaii or travel to the moon in a space shuttle, which would you choose, and why?

22. Where do you see yourself in 5 (10, 15) years? What will you be doing?

23. What would you do to make the world a better place?

24. What are three things that I should know about you? Explain each.

References
and Resources

• • •

Hundreds of books are available to guide teaching and inform instruction. The following provide rich information, support the ideas of this book, and include proven strategies and guidelines to advance teacher expertise and student learning.

Beck, I. L., McKeown, M. G., & Kucan, L. (2008). *Creating robust vocabulary.* New York: Guilford Press.

Great ideas and strategies for enriching vocabulary instruction for all ages.

Blachowicz, C., & Fisher, P. J. (2006). *Teaching vocabulary in all classrooms.* Upper Saddle River, NJ: Pearson/Merrill Prentice Hall.

Continuing ideas for vocabulary instruction for all ages; great, engaging activities.

Bloom, B. S., et al. (1956). *Taxonomy of educational objectives: The classification of educational goals.* New York: McKay.

Bonwell, C. C., & Eison, J. A. (1991). *Active learning: Creating excitement in the classroom.* Hoboken, NJ: Wiley.

Fun strategies for engaging, active learning.

Covey, S. A. (1995). *The 7 habits of highly effective people.* New York: Simon & Schuster.

Seven simple steps to help you become competent and effective in your life.

Dragan, P. B. (2005). *A how-to guide for teaching English language learners.* Portsmouth, NH: Heinemann.

Ideas for working with second language learners to scaffold their learning.

Dweck, C. S. (2006). *Mindset: The new psychology of success.* New York: Random House.

How a growth mind-set establishes successful outlook for teachers, students, and more.

Echevarria, J., Vogt, M., & Short, D. J. (2009). *Making comprehensible input for elementary English learners: The SIOP model.* Boston: Allyn & Bacon.
Ideas to support all learners.

Fisher, D., & Frey, N. (2007). *Checking for understanding: Formative assessment techniques for your classroom.* Alexandria, VA: ASCD.
Excellent ways to check that students know and understand the concepts you are teaching.

Gardner, H. (2007). *Responsibility at work.* San Francisco: John Wiley & Sons.
Ideas for reinforcing individual responsibility in personal and professional life.

Garner, B. K. (2007). *Getting to got it!* Alexandria, VA: ASCD.
Many great tips for helping students to learn and to become independent in their studies.

Graves, D. H. (1999). *Bring life into learning.* Portsmouth, NH: Heinemann.
Tips for firing up teaching and learning.

Harmon, J. M., Wood, K. D., & Hedrick, W. B. (2006). *Instructional strategies for teaching content vocabulary grades 4–12.* Newark, DE: International Reading Association.
Describes instructional strategies that support upper-elementary and secondary students.

Jones, F. (2000). *Tools for teaching.* Santa Cruz, CA: Fredric H. Jones & Associates Inc.
Ideas for making the classroom work effectively.

Marzano, R. J. (2007). *The art and science of teaching.* Alexandria, VA: ASCD.
Research-based models for improving many aspects of instruction and student learning.

Marzano, R. J., Pickering, D. J., & Pollock, J. E. (2001). *Classroom instruction that works: Research-based strategies for increasing student achievement.* Alexandria, VA: ASCD.
Key learning and engagement strategies explained, with a valuable section on meaningful feedback.

McTighe, J., & Wiggins, G. (1999). *The understanding by design handbook.* Alexandria, VA: ASCD.
Envisioning the end result means all steps of planning for instruction and assessment are on target, sequential, and clear.

Ogle, D. (1989). "The Know, Want to Know, Learn Strategy." In K. D. Muth (Ed.), *Children's comprehension of text: Research into practice* (pp. 205–223). Newark, DE: International Reading Association.

Owocki, G. (2003). *Comprehension: Strategic instruction for K–3 students.* Portsmouth, NH: Heinemann.
Many ideas that, although intended for elementary students, can be modified for building comprehension with students of any age.

Pollock, J. E. (2007). *Improving student learning one teacher at a time.* Alexandria, VA: ASCD.
Tips for improving student proficiency through excellence in teaching.

Popham, W. J. (2003). *Test better, teach better: The instructional role of assessment.* Alexandria, VA: ASCD.
Many tips for selecting the right test to gather the right data and knowing what to do with the results.

Sprenger, M. (2005). *How to teach so students remember.* Alexandria, VA: ASCD.
Tips for creating meaningful learning that goes beyond memorizing facts.

Stiggins, R., Arter, J. A., Chappuis, J., & Chappuis, S. (2004). Classroom assessment for student learning: Doing it right—using it well [conference]. Portland, OR: Assessment Training Institute.
Clarifies misconceptions about assessment and assessment design to help teachers create tests that reveal student understanding.

Stronge, J. H., Tucker, P. D., & Hindman, J. L. (2004). *Handbook of qualities of effective teachers.* Alexandria, VA: ASCD.
Great tips and ideas for becoming an effective teacher using high-quality instruction.

Thompson, J. G. (2007). *First year teacher's survival guide: Ready-to-use strategies, tools, and activities for meeting the challenge of each school day.* San Francisco: Jossey-Bass.
Tips for success to help new teachers teach more efficiently.

Whitaker, T. (2004). *What great teachers do differently: 14 things that matter most.* Larchmont, NY: Eye on Education.
Ideas to help teachers adjust lessons and instruction to make both more effective.

Wong, H. K., & Wong, R. T. (2004). *First days of school: How to be an effective teacher.* Mountain View, CA: Harry K. Wong Publications.
Information on launching a teaching career, especially during the first critical days on the job.

I've listed some of my favorite online resources. Also go to the Web sites of your school, district, and state department of education for critical information you need to know, as well as information about teaching and learning expectations and responsibilities.

rubistar.4teachers.org
Rubrics and ideas to support grading student work.

school.discovery.com
Ideas for lessons, discipline, and teaching resources.

www.ascd.org
Source of programs, products, and services for teachers, teacher leaders, and educators at all levels, K–16, including free study guides for books.

www.meggin.com
Ideas for engaging students and improving instruction; teleseminars, webinars, and downloadable products for busy teachers.

www.lessonplanspage.com
Ideas for lesson plans.

www.lessonplanz.com
More ideas for lesson plans.

www.nea.org
Teaching resources and ideas for lessons and discipline.

www2.scholastic.com
More teaching resources and ideas for lessons and discipline.

Index

The letter *f* following a page number denotes a figure.

About the Author

● ● ●

Gini Cunningham

After 28 years in the classroom, I jumped at the opportunity to extend my knowledge and skills by becoming a regional coordinator in professional development. My years with students, kindergarten through college, plus the additional time spent in observation, collaboration, and teaching model lessons with hundreds of teachers and thousands of students have provided me with the background and firsthand information to enable me to share my excitement for learning.

I have always wanted to know more about everything. From my bachelor's degree in French and physical education to a master's degree in literacy plus National Board Certification in English/language arts, every educational challenge has been met with enthusiasm and a desire to improve my skills. This book is the product of a lifetime of learning and experience. Everything is tried and true and will support all teachers and their instruction.

I continue to extend my knowledge daily by working in class-rooms with students and teaching professionals and administrators. I pass educational tips on to parents through a monthly newspaper column. My next writing projects include guides for mentor-teachers and developing a love of writing across grade levels and the curriculum.

I can be reached by e-mail at gini.cunningham@sbcglobal.net; or visit my Web site, www.energizedlearning.net.